THE PSYCHOLOGY OF GOD

Ten Sons of Haman

LM McCormick

Disclaimer

The author of this work has quoted the writers of many articles and books. This does not mean that the author endorses or recommends the works of others. If the author quotes someone, it does not mean that she agrees with all of the author's tenets, statements, concepts, or words, whether in the work quoted or any other work of the author. There has been no attempt to alter the meaning of the quotes; and therefore, some of the quotes are long in order to give the entire sense of the passage.

Copyrighted © by LM McCormick

REL006201: Religion: Biblical Studies - Topical

ISBN 978-0-9993545-6-8

All Scripture quotes are from the King James Bible except those verses compared and then the source is identified.

No part of this work may be reproduced without the expressed consent of the publisher, except for brief quotes, whether by electronic, photocopying, recording, or information storage and retrieval systems.

Address All Inquiries To:
THE OLD PATHS PUBLICATIONS, Inc.
142 Gold Flume Way
Cleveland, Georgia, U.S.A.

Web: www.theoldpathspublications.com
E-mail: TOP@theoldpathspublications.com

DEDICATION

This book is dedicated to Chuck Missler, whose teachings have taught so many, including myself. I would also like to thank my husband and editor, Ted, for all his patience and love, and for a fine editing job. And to my mother and father, who were always so generous in every way, and gave me the understanding I needed, to know that I was a writer at heart.

If he were here, I'd also like to thank my friend, Doug Milburn, for having the faith in me to write a book together. Unfortunately, Doug went to be with his Lord just as the book was getting started. Lord, bless him. I'd also like to thank my sister Diane, who spent time teaching me how to write when I was a kid. And my sister Ann, who always had an ear for me whenever I needed. God bless all of you.

LM McCormick

THE PSYCHOLOGY OF GOD: TEN SONS OF HAMAN

PROLOGUE

This book begins with a Bible story, a story that ends with the death of the family of a very wicked man who was plotting against Israel. His name was Haman, and he was the architect of the destruction of the Jews. As the plan goes wrong, the sons of Haman are killed. All ten sons.

Then, a mysterious twist occurs. The ten sons of Haman, who are already dead, are ordered by Queen Esther to be hung "tomorrow" (Esther 9:11-14). Why would the queen ask to hang the dead?

You might notice that the Hebrew names of Haman's sons are similar in nature; the meanings in themselves are composed of "self" reference. Self-righteous, weak self, and bold self are examples. And as we dig deeper into the list of ten, we see negative human personality traits such as gossiping, being headstrong, having false humility, being a bully, and other character flaws, all named within each of these dead, and hung, sons of Haman.

What the uninitiated do not understand is that within these names are characteristics that describe the enemies of God.

This first book of *The Psychology of God, "Ten Sons of Haman,"* is a glimpse into the great healing power of God as He reveals His knowledge of the human spirit, to help His children understand the exact ways in which they miss the mark of Christ.

Inside this book you'll discover the individual meanings of the names of the dead sons of Haman, and the sinful traits they stand for. You will discover that these names are the antithesis of the love God asks us to bestow upon our neighbor. We'll also look at these traits in other places in the Bible, and their history.

Let me suggest that you look at the list of names in their entirety, in the Introduction section, before you start studying the names themselves individually.

The first time I saw the meaning of the sons' names, it knocked the breath out of me. It just astounded me speechless that God knows us so intimately that He can name these aspects of human nature so accurately. God directly confronts the evil that resides inside mankind by naming these traits, exposing the negative tendencies that we even hide from ourselves. And then, He provides a cure for us – with prayer, recognizing His love for us, knowing Him, trusting Him, following Him. By doing that, we can overcome these temptations to act sinfully.

The description hidden in the names of the *ten sons of Haman* are *traits we want to avoid, as God's children*. This proves that the Word of God can heal our very spirit as He shapes our nature to be more like Jesus. People who merely touched Jesus' hem were instantly cured; and remember, Jesus is "the Word made Flesh." Wouldn't it also make sense that when we take the Word within us, know it, making it a part of us, that His perfection, becomes ours, and heals us?

If Jesus is truly the Word made Flesh, God's Word from His mouth, then when we learn the Bible and commit it to our memory, He becomes a part of us. This part no man can take away from us. And

PROLOGUE

this is how "Jesus lives in you." It is how God Himself lives within you, by the Word, and the Holy Spirit, within you. How comforting is this thought to you? Doesn't it make sense that following Jesus, and staying within the Word of God, would naturally heal people's depressed, lost, or confused spirits?

When we see the Bible show us such insight into human nature, it tells us more secrets are in the scriptures, just waiting for us to find them. We already know we can count on the Word to tell us what's coming; thousands of biblical prophecies that have unfolded, over thousands of years, prove this beyond any doubt. But we can also count on it today, because the Word of God is prescriptive. *Ten Sons of Haman* gives us a hint of what is stored inside the Word of God for us to learn about ourselves, about the human spirit that is within every human being, directly from our Creator.

We all know the Bible demonstrates repeatedly that we should trust in God, that He keeps all His promises, and teaches us that He is faithful, patient, and long-suffering; these are eternal, loving, healing words. In my opinion, they are the most comforting words on the earth, that God loves us more than we can comprehend, and that we can trust Him to put our best interests first.

What is more healing than learning our ultimate purpose is from our very own Creator? Learning in our hearts about who made us, who knows us best, and how He loves us completely, eternally, and unconditionally? That the work for our salvation has already been done? How much more soothing for people suffering from depression, anger, guilt, and such, is it to know we have God's eternal favor, rather than man's, which is so fickle, and will pass away? And a love so solid and deep that we do not deserve, that we can hardly comprehend it. Hearing these words can be better than any prescription from a pharmacy. Today's secular counselors, psychologists, psychiatrists, and therapists, do not deal with sin and evil, which are problems everyone has in life to some degree. Instead, everything is discussed and defined in terms of "illness," disorder and disease. This not only sets up an environment where everyone is 'sick' but even more importantly, that "nobody is healthy." Definitions must be constantly re-written when the foundations are on shifting sand (the DSM-5 continues to re-name and re-define mental illness). Conversely, the doctor or counselor who leans upon the Rock has wisdom that never changes. The Word of God was the same yesterday as it is today and will be tomorrow, always the same godly wisdom that is specifically designed to help Man with his problems of the heart, mind, and spirit.

My contention is that, with faith, we can watch God heal everything from the deepest loss and sorrow and failure, to many of our physical 'disorders,' using the Bible as the main tool of reference. The knowledge of man is on shifting sand. But our education, from Holy Scripture, is built on Rock. It is truth that never changes.

The account of the ten sons of Haman is just a tiny snowflake in a winter storm of clues hidden within the pages of the Word of God. And we are thankful to the Lord we have been given this

PROLOGUE

blessing. I leave it to you, dear reader, to uncover more secrets.

If you feel you'd like to write about it, expand it, add examples from scripture or from your own practice, and wish to share it, feel free to write to me if it pleases you. Although I write, and speak, I am neither a preacher nor a teacher, but just a woman who loves God.

God's blessings to you.

LM McCormick

TABLE OF CONTENTS

DEDICATION 3
PROLOGUE 5
TABLE OF CONTENTS 11
INTRODUCTION 13
CHAPTER 1 19
The First Son - The Busybody 19
CHAPTER 2 37
The Second Son - The Sad Sack 37
CHAPTER 3 47
The Third Son - The Self-Made Man 47
CHAPTER 4 53
The Fourth Son - The Party Animal 53
CHAPTER 5 65
The Fifth Son - The Snowflake 65
CHAPTER 6 73
The Sixth Son - The Bully 73
CHAPTER 7 85
The Seventh Son - The Narcissist 85
CHAPTER 8 93
The Eighth Son - The Over-Confident One .. 93
CHAPTER 9 103
The Ninth Son - The Arrogant One 103

CHAPTER 10	**109**
The Tenth Son - The Pharisee	**109**
EPILOGUE	**115**
INDEX OF WORDS AND PHRASES	**119**
ABOUT THE AUTHOR	**123**

INTRODUCTION

THE SONS OF HAMAN. KILLED, THEN HUNG.

Thousands of years ago, a man named Haman, an evil and corrupt government official, plotted to kill all the Jews. His plan backfired, due to the efforts of Queen Esther and her cousin, a good Jew named Mordecai. Jews worldwide celebrate this victory every year in the feast of Purim.

In this Bible story, in the Book of Esther, the sons of Haman were not simply killed - after they were killed, they were then hung, by the Queen's request. So, in a sense, they were each killed twice, even if one of them is symbolic.

What is the significance of this, and how did it happen in scripture? Let's revisit the original story.

Esther 9:11-14

> *11 On that day the number of those that were slain in Shushan the palace was brought before the king. 12 And the king said unto Esther the queen, The Jews have slain and destroyed five hundred men in Shushan the palace, and the ten sons of Haman; what have they done in the rest of the king's provinces? now what is thy petition? and it shall be granted thee: or what is thy request further? and it shall be done. 13 Then said Esther, If it please the king, let it be granted to the Jews which are in Shushan to do to morrow also according unto this day's*

> *decree, and let Haman's ten sons be hanged upon the gallows. 14 And the king commanded it so to be done: and the decree was given at Shushan; and they hanged Haman's ten sons.*

The king agrees to the Queen's request, and the dead sons are hanged.

The mystery as to why Queen Esther would ask to hang the ten sons of Haman on the gallows after they were already dead, is a matter of deeper study. One must understand that the definition of the word "morrow" (KJV) meaning "tomorrow" in modern times, perhaps has a different meaning here - that it means "the tomorrow that is today, and the tomorrow in the future." By this logic, scholars claim that the ten men hanged in Nuremberg for their crimes against Jews during Hitler's time are a fulfillment of this prophecy:

In Esther 3:1, we are told that Haman was an Agagite. Agag was the king of Amalek (1 Sam. 15:8). Therefore, Haman and his sons were Amalekites. These are the grandsons of Esau, whom God "hated."

Thousands of years later, Rabbi Elijah Solomon, a prominent Lithuanian rabbi of the 18th century, known as "the great one of Vilna," held the tradition that the German nation was descended from the Amalekites. During World War II, the Nazis in Germany tried to wipe the Jewish race from the face of the earth. Six million Jews were

INTRODUCTION

killed by the Germans, but they failed in their plan to annihilate them all.

After the end of the war, the surviving Nazi leaders were tried at Nuremberg for this and other war crimes. These trials for twenty-two German Nazi leaders began on November 20, 1945. On October 1, 1946, twelve of the German defendants were sentenced to death by hanging for their part in the atrocities committed against the Jews and others. One of those convicted was Martin Bormann, who was sentenced in absentia. A second was Hermann Goering, who committed suicide in his cell just hours before the executions by taking cyanide poison.

The remaining ten Germans were hanged to death on October 16, 1946. Is this the "tomorrow" fulfillment of God's prophecy, in the story of Haman's sons?

When I look at this scripture in Esther, with the bizarre request to hang dead men, I imagine that God might have wanted the world to see that the ten sons of Haman stood for something greater, more meaningful even than just the evil actions of Haman against the Jews; that in fact, the meaning of their names was something God wanted to "die" or extinguish from every human personality. In fact, the natures of the names of these ten sons are the personal attributes of the enemies of God.

Haman, who was an evil, powerful man, was a high official in the Persian Empire. He was a man who hated the Jews and tried to exterminate them all because one Jew wouldn't pay homage. Mordecai, a Jew, would not bow down to Haman. Instead of taking vengeance on Mordecai, Haman instead sought to destroy every single Jew throughout the Persian kingdom. The result was the death of his ten sons, and their names are listed below. His failure is recorded in the 9th book of Esther:

Esther 9:1-10

> *Now in the twelfth month, that is, the month Adar, on the thirteenth day of the same, when the king's commandment and his decree drew near to be put in execution, in the day that the enemies of the Jews hoped to have power over them, (though it was turned to the contrary, that the Jews had rule over them that hated them;) The Jews gathered themselves together in their cities throughout all the provinces of the king Ahasuerus, to lay hand on such as sought their hurt: and no man could withstand them; for the fear of them fell upon all people. And all the rulers of the provinces, and the lieutenants, and the deputies, and officers of the king, helped the Jews; because the fear of Mordecai fell upon them. For Mordecai was great in the king's house, and his fame went out throughout all the provinces: for this man Mordecai waxed greater and greater. Thus the Jews smote all their enemies with the stroke of the sword, and slaughter, and destruction, and did what they would unto those that hated them. And in Shushan the*

INTRODUCTION

palace the Jews slew and destroyed five hundred men. And Parshandatha, and Dalphon, and Aspatha, And Poratha, and Adalia, and Aridatha, And Parmashta, and Arisai, and Aridai, and Vajezatha, The ten sons of Haman the son of Hammedatha, the enemy of the Jews, slew they; but on the spoil laid they not their hand.

Here are the ten names, in order, that we will discuss throughout this book, in a handy list:

Son	Name	Meaning
1st	Parshandatha	Curious Self - "busybody"
2nd	Dalphon	Weeping Self - "self-pity"
3rd	Aspatha	Assembled Self -"self-mobilized," "self-sufficiency"
4th	Poratha	Generous Self - "spend-thriftiness", "self-indulgence"
5th	Adalia	Weak Self - "self-consciousness", "inferiority"
6th	Aridatha	Strong Self - "assertiveness", "insists upon one's way"
7th	Parmashta	Preeminent Self - "ambitious", "desire for preeminence"
8th	Arisai	Bold Self - "imprudent"
9th	Aridai	Dignified Self - "prideful", "haughty", "sense of superiority"
10th	Vajezatha	Pure Self - "self-righteousness" (considered worst of all)

The next ten chapters describe biblical and psychological aspects of each of these names. It is not exhaustive but gives us a starting point to discuss these personality traits. Note that all the names begin with "self." It appears to be an identifier of the negativity of these concepts, something inside the self, inside the human personality, that is to be purged or altered.

From gossiping to self-righteousness, the names of the ten sons of Haman reveal personality flaws that represent a fascinating glimpse into the little clues and keys that God puts as breadcrumbs through scripture, leading us further into the refining process of us, as His children, in our understanding, and in our very natures.

Now, let's take a look at each one of these names, and their deeper meanings, and what else the Bible has to say about them. Let's start in Chapter One with "The Busybody," the man whose name means "I am curious."

CHAPTER 1

The First Son - The Busybody

The first of Haman's ten sons to die is known as "Arshandatha," which means the "Curious" Self, or, "I am Curious."

What does it mean to be "curious"? Why would God kill this attribute twice? Like many of the names of the sons of Haman, there is a positive as well as a negative connotation of the word curious. As we think about an overabundance of curiosity, we can surmise even by the old saying, "curiosity killed the cat" that curiosity and death are associated.

A certain amount of curiosity in one's life isn't such a terrible thing. It leads some people to the study of science and other realms of knowledge, including the Bible. And the best kind of curiosity is about God's Word. So why would God select it as an aspect of human personality that He feels must change or end, symbolized in the death of this particular name, "Curiosity"? Why list it as a trait of His enemies?

The first aspect of an overabundance of curiosity is the ungodly personality trait of being a "busybody," poking our noses into other people's business where it doesn't belong. Busybodies naturally judge others, not noticing the beam in their own eye, while pointing out the mote in their brothers' or sisters' eyes.

In fact, the old saying about that cat with the curiosity seems more addressed to human beings than to felines, given its usage in times when people are too curious about other people's affairs. What's worse is that a surplus of curiosity can lead to gossip, which "curious ears" would always like to hear, and it is surely a negative, ungodly practice when others go around talking about other people's intimate business.

Point in fact that scripture tells us that a woman under 62 years of age, who becomes a widow, is to marry again. Why? So she won't become a 'busybody,' poking her nose in other people's business:

1 Timothy 5:13

> *And withal they learn to be idle, wandering about from house to house; and not only idle, but tattlers also and busybodies, speaking things which they ought not.*

Gossip magazines and shows are also good examples of a human's natural curiosity about other humans. It's hard not to peek at those gossipy headlines going out of the grocery store check-out, isn't it?

Thinking further, an excess of curiosity could easily lead Christians into all manner of deviant and

CHAPTER 1: THE FIRST SON - THE BUSYBODY

despicable views of mankind's practices, including the occult.

Starting with a curiosity towards astrology, and the black arts such as Ouija boards, tarot cards, crystals, and the like, curious Christians sometimes just want to "try something new" or "explore." This is code for indulging their sin, with their curiosity about these dark matters often leading to disastrous results, opening a dimensional gateway to Satan and his hateful minions. There have been many destroyed marriages and careers because of such so-called "dabbling."

The X-rated movie *"I am Curious Yellow"* also comes to mind about the curious sexual nature of the deviant. In *"Fifty Shades of Gray,"* the woman is curious about the perverse nature of a fornicator. Hollywood is the Accuser's mouthpiece. Satan will use anything against God's people that he can, and TV and film shape the mind of youth more than any other force in our society. Government-run public schools unfortunately reinforce these ungodly values. The founder of the Satanic church, Anton Le Vey, knew this. He said the TV would do the work for him. Satan has known man for thousands of years. He knows how to coat things with sugar to entice the willing to swallow his lies easily. Anyone who thinks they can outsmart Satan are ignoring the Bible which says that He fools the whole world.

Many of these distractions from the Evil One begin with an innocent-sounding "I wonder if..."

and lead the Christian, especially the young Christian, down a road of earthly creations that go into everything from perversion of sexual practices, even to movie superheroes, and New World Order religion. These practices and religions are often dressed up as charitable and "peaceful" *(man's peace, not God's Peace) but have an underbelly of perversion and corruption that the unsuspecting do not see. There are none that I have ever encountered who don't regret this dark path sooner or later.

The Enemy is so crafty as even to turn the Christian cross upside down, break the arms of Jesus, and thus create the Peace symbol. If you don't believe that's true, go look up the history of it. This is how subtle and ubiquitous the opposition is. Have you noticed that the Peace symbol is having a big resurgence lately, all over the place, in clothing and textiles?

Church attendance in the United States has dropped to a depressing 25% and we wonder why? In the Word of God it is prophesied that our brethren will no longer endure sound doctrine, they will have itching ears for the doctrines of devils, and that there will be a "great falling away" from the truth. It's happening now. The true Bible-believing Christian can see it happening all around him. And we see that part of the root of this is because of repeated temptations in society to be "curious" about reprobate activities such as perverted sex, drugs, and drunkenness. These promote a rebellious nature, blur the lines between

CHAPTER 1: THE FIRST SON - THE BUSYBODY

God's creation of men and women, and destroy the covenant of marriage, given by God. The Enemy wants most of all to destroy everything that God holds dear.

Eventually many Christians begin to question the authority of God because of seeing too many of these distractions. In their curious exploration of Arianism, secularism, and paganism, embodied in cults and wayward churches, many have turned from the truth - which is the Enemy's purpose. We are seeing the "great falling away" of people from God, from His Son who created all this world, the Word made Flesh, the Spotless Lamb. And if you study the Word you know it says that Jesus cannot return until this "falling away" has occurred, so we praise Him that His Word is coming to pass.

2 Timothy 4:3

> *For the time will come when they will not endure the sound doctrine; but, having itching ears, will heap to themselves teachers after their own lusts.*

2 Thessalonians 2:1-4

> *Now we beseech you, brethren, by the coming of our Lord Jesus Christ, and by our gathering together unto him, That ye be not soon shaken in mind, or be troubled, neither by spirit, nor by word, nor by letter as from us, as that the day of Christ is at hand. Let no man deceive you by any means: for that day shall not come, except there come a falling away first, and that man of sin be*

> *revealed, the son of perdition; Who opposeth and exalteth himself above all that is called God, or that is worshipped; so that he as God sitteth in the temple of God, shewing himself that he is God.*

So curiosity is very often the first step in falling headlong into cult and occult practices. It's why Satan has placed so many religions in the world, to confuse believers and non-believers alike and to believe what Adam and Eve, the first human beings on this planet, believed when they heard the snake. It starts with curiosity and then leads into the lies about God, and being unknowledgeable like Eve, we begin to doubt our own faith. Eve believed for a moment that God is a liar and that He doesn't have our best interests at heart. She believed that God didn't want to "share" His godlike ability with her; Satan convinced her that she could "Be like God" the way that Satan wants to be. Today, many religions tell people that Jesus isn't the only way to God, when Jesus clearly said, *"No man cometh unto to the Father, but by me."* (John 14:6)

One of Lucifer's distractions is to use old myths to try to say that "the story of Jesus has happened before." Counterfeit ancient stories that supposedly mimic the story of Jesus, such as the Egyptian story of Horus, for example, lead the overly curious to question the deity and truth of Christ. The thing is, if they really studied this Horus myth, they'd see that the story isn't anywhere like the story of Jesus. A quick review shows no real comparison. They are reaching hard for any so-called "evidence" that would lead them away from Christ, since a cursory examination of the two

CHAPTER 1: THE FIRST SON - THE BUSYBODY

stories yields a tremendous stretch to make Horus into a Jesus figure.

These people who argue this point want you to deny the fact that Jesus taught repeatedly throughout scripture that He is God. The Pharisees certainly understood what Jesus was saying:

John 10:31-32

> *Then the Jews took up stones again to stone him. Jesus answered them, Many good works have I shewed you from my Father; for which of those works do ye stone me?*
>
> *The Jews answered him, saying, for a good work we stone thee not; but for blasphemy; and because that thou, being a man, makest thyself God."*

In fact, *"He maketh Himself God"* was the official charge against Him, which to the religious Jew meant blasphemy, a mortal crime - and it led Him to the cross at the hands of the Romans by the beseeching of the Pharisees. It is a historical and scientific fact that Jesus lived, and died upon that cross.

It's so strange to me when I see so-called Christians being curious about "other religions," because, if they study, they will find "other religions" ignore all the places where He said He was one with the Most High, ("*I and my Father are one*"). They fall into whatever excuse the new religion gives for disbelieving this fact and rejecting the truth that Jesus will return as He said. This is "new age religion"; a rejection of what scripture teaches.

Another rejection of this 'new age' religion is that hell, which He spoke of often, "isn't real." "Everybody goes to heaven" is their belief, which negates any sense of true justice. But in a new world order where every participant gets an award just for being there, the One World Religion certainly will not mention hell.

Too few in the world understand where all the religions come from. Hinduism is a great example. Fallen angels (demons), who left their heavenly abode, quickly set up false religions to worship themselves, one of them being to set up worship of themselves as "gods" in Hinduism. One can easily see the Spirit of Jezebel, for example, or the Spirit of Satan, and the Spirit of Death, in the overt symbolism of the so-called "gods" of Hinduism, clearly presented in the statues and drawings which contain severed heads, blue deathly skin, human bones, and as always - snakes. Hindu scriptures also contain a fascinating account of nuclear war; it appears the "gods" (fallen angels/demons) were warring with each other after they fell from their first estate. The descriptions of these events are amazing in the Hindu texts.

Along with the worship of the sun, snakes are represented in one form or another (sometimes as dragons, which can also be references to dinosaurs) in pretty much all false religions, and you'll find them all over the world, in all ancient

CHAPTER 1: THE FIRST SON - THE BUSYBODY

cultures. No one has to tell even the most backslid Christian what snakes stand for.

Satan always reveals himself in these ancient religions. One look at the snake on the crowns of the ancient Egyptian artifacts tells you of its prominence. See the snake on the head of the Sphinx, and its relationship to the pyramids. The erotic art that is emblazoned in some of these precious antiques tells you a lot about what their society was about. There's no accident that there were serpents right at the top of their crowns.

Curiosity can also lead people into the belief in aliens, UFOs, or other "curiosities" such as ghost hunting, astral projection and other metaphysical phenomenon. Some of these practices and beliefs can open the dimensional channels to demons who wish to lead humans who are ignorant and Christians who are "curious" away from the focus on Jesus.

Evidence exists in the fact that even secular researchers of UFO phenomenon have noted that calling upon the name of Jesus "makes the abduction experience suddenly cease." It appears that these "aliens" are simply more of the fallen ones who want to lead human beings astray by posing as extraterrestrial beings. False religions, aliens, "ghosts," and other phenomenon are these fallen beings making fools of human beings.

There is nothing you can "contact" outside the human realm that is a "good" spirit. They are all bad, evil entities that have betrayed God and hope to keep you from entering heaven. The Bible says that soothsayers, those who practice magic, will not enter heaven.

This is what the Bible says about "soothsaying" (witchcraft):

Leviticus 19:26

> *Ye shall not eat any thing with the blood: neither shall ye use enchantment, nor observe times.*

Leviticus 19:31

> *Regard not them that have familiar spirits, neither seek after wizards, to be defiled by them: I am the LORD your God.*

Leviticus 20:6

> *And the soul that turneth after such as have familiar spirits, and after wizards, to go a whoring after them, I will even set my face against that soul, and will cut him off from among his people. (see also Leviticus 20:27)*

Deuteronomy 18:10-14

> *There shall not be found among you any one that maketh his son or his daughter to pass through the fire, or that useth divination, or an observer of times, or an enchanter, or a witch, Or a charmer, or a consulter with familiar spirits, or a wizard, or a necromancer. For all that do these things are an abomination unto the LORD: and*

CHAPTER 1: THE FIRST SON - THE BUSYBODY

> *because of these abominations the LORD thy God doth drive them out from before thee. Thou shalt be perfect with the LORD thy God. For these nations, which thou shalt possess, hearkened unto observers of times, and unto diviners: but as for thee, the LORD thy God hath not suffered thee so to do.*

Micah 5:12

> *And I will cut off witchcrafts out of thine hand; and thou shalt have no more soothsayers:*

Revelation 21:8

> *But the fearful, and unbelieving, and the abominable, and murderers, and whoremongers, and sorcerers, and idolaters, and all liars, shall have their part in the lake which burneth with fire and brimstone: which is the second death.*

One of the threads throughout the Bible is about the "signs" of Jesus' coming, and how people demanded signs from Him as to His deity. Signs in general are throughout the scriptures by the thousands. Knowing Jesus' identity as the Son of God and Messiah was based on these signs known as "biblical prophecy." Signs such as the Bethlehem star that the "wise men" followed, or Jesus being born in Bethlehem, or riding into Jerusalem on a donkey were all prophetic utterances. The prophetic sign came from a prophet, who would make a statement or prediction about the future, and later, the statement would come true.

Following is the prophetic example regarding Jesus riding into the city of Jerusalem, on a donkey:

First the Old Testament prophecy:

Zechariah 9:9

> *Rejoice greatly, O daughter of Zion; shout, O daughter of Jerusalem: behold, thy King cometh unto thee: he is just, and having salvation; lowly, and riding upon an ass, and upon a colt the foal of an ass.*

Then the New Testament realization of Zechariah's prophecy from 600 years earlier:

Mark 11:1-10

> *"And when they came nigh to Jerusalem, unto Bethphage and Bethany, at the mount of Olives, he sendeth forth two of his disciples, And saith unto them, Go your way into the village over against you: and as soon as ye be entered into it, ye shall find a colt tied, whereon never man sat; loose him, and bring him. And if any man say unto you, Why do ye this? say ye that the Lord hath need of him; and straightway he will send him hither. And they went their way, and found the colt tied by the door without in a place where two ways met; and they loose him. And certain of them that stood there said unto them, What do ye, loosing the colt? And they said unto them even as Jesus had commanded: and*

CHAPTER 1: THE FIRST SON - THE BUSYBODY

they let them go. And they brought the colt to Jesus, and cast their garments on him; and he sat upon him. And many spread their garments in the way: and others cut down branches off the trees, and strawed them in the way. And they that went before, and they that followed, cried, saying, Hosanna; Blessed is he that cometh in the name of the Lord: Blessed be the kingdom of our father David, that cometh in the name of the Lord: Hosanna in the highest."

Matthew 21:1-11

And when they drew nigh unto Jerusalem, and were come to Bethphage, unto the mount of Olives, then sent Jesus two disciples, Saying unto them, Go into the village over against you, and straightway ye shall find an ass tied, and a colt with her: loose them, and bring them unto me. And if any man say ought unto you, ye shall say, The Lord hath need of them; and straightway he will send them. All this was done, that it might be fulfilled which was spoken by the prophet, saying, Tell ye the daughter of Sion, Behold, thy King cometh unto thee, meek, and sitting upon an ass, and a colt the foal of an ass. And the disciples went, and did as Jesus commanded them, And brought the ass, and the colt, and put on them their clothes, and they set him thereon. And a very great multitude spread their garments in the way; others cut down branches from the trees, and strawed them in the way. And the multitudes that went before, and that

> *followed, cried, saying, Hosanna to the Son of David: Blessed is he that cometh in the name of the Lord; Hosanna in the highest. And when he was come into Jerusalem, all the city was moved, saying, Who is this? And the multitude said, This is Jesus the prophet of Nazareth of Galilee.*

The Bible contains, by some counts, close to 2,000 prophesies, the vast majority of which have already been fulfilled.

Dear Reader, these fulfilled prophecies are miracles, and one of the proofs of God's existence, and the veracity of the Bible. You will find upon great scrutiny that the Bible is the real Word of God, breathed out from the mouth of your Creator, and that the scriptures are completely inerrant. Jesus is the Word made Flesh; and so the Word is as perfect as HE is.

Curiosity is also associated with the natural seeking of these signs, as Ecclesiastes 1:8 tells us that the human mind has a curiosity that is never really satisfied, and this is expressed in the fervent seeking of signs. The Bible speaks of this in the following scriptures that you might like to contemplate:

Ecclesiastes 1:8

> *All things are full of labour; man cannot utter it: the eye is not satisfied with seeing, nor the ear filled with hearing.*

CHAPTER 1: THE FIRST SON - THE BUSYBODY

John 12:9

Much people of the Jews therefore knew that he was there: and they came not for Jesus' sake only, but that they might see Lazarus also, whom he had raised from the dead.

Acts 17:21

(For all the Athenians and strangers which were there spent their time in nothing else, but either to tell, or to hear some new thing.)

Matthew 12:38

Then certain of the scribes and of the Pharisees answered, saying, Master, we would see a sign from thee.

Matthew 16:1

The Pharisees also with the Sadducees came, and tempting desired him that he would shew them a sign from heaven.

Matthew 24:3

And as he sat upon the mount of Olives, the disciples came unto him privately, saying, Tell us, when shall these things be? and what shall be the sign of thy coming, and of the end of the world?

Mark 8:11

And the Pharisees came forth, and began to question with him, seeking of him a sign from heaven, tempting him.

Luke 11:6

For a friend of mine in his journey is come to me, and I have nothing to set before him?

John 2:18

Then answered the Jews and said unto him, What sign shewest thou unto us, seeing that thou doest these things?"

John 4:48

Then said Jesus unto him, Except ye see signs and wonders, ye will not believe.

John 6:30

They said therefore unto him, What sign shewest thou then, that we may see, and believe thee? what dost thou work?

1 Corinthians 1:22

For the Jews require a sign, and the Greeks seek after wisdom:

Ecclesiastes 1:8

All things are full of labour; man cannot utter it: the eye is not satisfied with seeing, nor the ear filled with hearing.

John 6:2

And a great multitude followed him, because they saw his miracles which he did on them that were diseased.

CHAPTER 1: THE FIRST SON - THE BUSYBODY

1 Peter 1:12

Unto whom it was revealed, that not unto themselves, but unto us they did minister the things, which are now reported unto you by them that have preached the gospel unto you with the Holy Ghost sent down from heaven; which things the angels desire to look into.

Proverbs 27:20

Hell and destruction are never full; so the eyes of man are never satisfied.

Acts 1:7

And he said unto them, It is not for you to know the times or the seasons, which the Father hath put in his own power.

CHAPTER 2

The Second Son - The Sad Sack

1 Thessalonians 5:16-18

Rejoice evermore. Pray without ceasing. In every thing give thanks: for this is the will of God in Christ Jesus concerning you.

The second son of Haman that was "killed twice" was named "Dalphon," which means "Weeping Self" or "Self-Pity." There's no positive spin on this meaning in terms of personality benefits.

It's safe to say that self-pity is one of the worst emotions one can have as a Christian. In fact, it's demonstrable that self-pity is the opposite of what God wants of us as His children, and not what Jesus taught His followers to practice. It is the continually depressed person, the "sad sack," who is in one's own misery without end. A sad sack never shows the joy of the Lord, and without exception spreads his or her misery to others.

First, Christ taught that we should be more concerned about others, more than we are about ourselves. And as we examine its properties, we see that really, self-pity is a form of selfishness. The dictionary defines "self-pity" as "a self-indulgent dwelling on your own sorrows or misfortune." Basically, it undermines biblical fundamental concepts such as being filled with the joy of knowing the Lord and "thankful in all circumstances" (1 Thessalonians 5:18). This includes limiting charity towards others, as we focus upon ourselves.

Secondly, being full of self-pity, asserts the idea that "life is unfair." That basically means that God is unfair, since He is the author of life. God is righteous, and never 'unfair.' Having pity upon ourselves skirts responsibility for our actions and states that "God got it wrong" in our lives, when, in reality, the Word of God teaches us that all things work for our good:

Romans 8:28

> *And we know that all things work together for good to them that love God, to them who are the called according to his purpose.*

Self-pity avoids taking some responsibility and bearing our own challenges or burdens. When one allows oneself to wallow in self-pity, it asserts to God, "I deserve a better life than you have dealt me." That in and of itself is extremely arrogant and disrespectful. It ignores or discounts the fact that there are others whose life circumstances might be much worse. And it dismisses what the Lord says about His plans for us, which are for good:

CHAPTER 2: THE SECOND SON - THE SAD SACK

Jeremiah 29:11

> *For I know the thoughts that I think toward you, saith the LORD, thoughts of peace, and not of evil, to give you an expected end.*

One can look to the story of Job as a great example of getting away from self-pity. If anyone had a reason to feel sorry for himself, it was he, yet Job kept reaching out to the Lord for answers. Job did this despite the urging of his neighbors, friends, and even his wife, who implored him to give up on God, and to simply die.

Job may have questioned God, but he waited for God to answer him. Self-pity is the end of hope. It puts forth the idea that we can do everything on our own, instead of showing dependence on God through prayer. It's the statement that God isn't fair, isn't loving, and we are somehow being 'punished'.

Thirdly, self-pity is a form of complaining to ourselves. God has made it clear in His Word that complaining is something that gives Him displeasure:

Numbers 11:1

> *And when the people complained, it displeased the LORD: and the LORD heard it; and his anger was kindled; and the fire of the LORD burnt among them, and consumed them that were in the uttermost parts of the camp.*

In Numbers 11, this is evident throughout the chapter; one example being how the Israelites complained about the lack of the exotic foods they had been given by the Egyptians. They lamented about that while they were in the desert, displeasing God, who arranged for their death through a plague. Pretty bad results for their self-pity!

And it's not just complaining that God dislikes. The product of self-pity is bitterness; this displeases God very much, and it causes His anger.

Ephesians 4:31-32

> *Let all bitterness and wrath and anger and clamor and slander be put away from you, along with all malice. Be kind to one another, tender-hearted, forgiving each other, just as God in Christ also has forgiven you.*

Lastly, self-pity often is a disguise for not forgiving others that might be responsible or partly at fault for our misfortune or misery. It is often a strategy to illicit guilt or assistance from other parties. In this passage in Ephesians we see our wise and blessed Lord has addressed this for us. It's a prescription for our lasting happiness.

The Bible says that when God forgives us, He "remembers our sin no more" (Jeremiah 31:34)

Self-pity and blame also can include oneself, in not forgiving ourselves for mistakes we have made,

CHAPTER 2: THE SECOND SON - THE SAD SACK

and that in itself denies the actual salvation from our sins by Jesus Christ's blood sacrifice.

1 Samuel 30:6

> *"And David was greatly distressed; for the people spoke of stoning him, because the soul of all the people was grieved, every man for his sons and for his daughters: but David encouraged himself in the LORD his God."*

Here David had every reason to be depressed. Let us remember when God took his son, he cried and fasted and prayed and prayed, but when he knew the child was dead and there was no changing it, he got up, bathed and ate, knowing there was nothing he could do. He had prayed fervently, beseeching His Lord, but now he was going to go on living.

Human beings generally come out stronger after adversity. We learn from mistakes. Self-pitying denies this kind of taking of responsibility, and milks the situation for attention. King David could have continued to wallow in his self-pity, but didn't. Mature Christians shouldn't allow this to happen, either. Serious Christians know how to look at the big picture, that this life will seem like a mere vapor in our future. We are just passing through this brief life on earth; our real home is in heaven. That fact should make the troubles of this world seem pale.

THE PSYCHOLOGY OF GOD: TEN SONS OF HAMAN

Psalm 118:6

The LORD is on my side; I will not fear: what can man do unto me?

Self-pity can also be addicting because of the attention it gets, and the associated comforting from others, which makes us feel better. We may become dependent on the whole process, and thus dependent on the depression and sorrow if it becomes habitual. Feeling sorry for oneself can be a "comfortable state" to stay in. But it isn't godly, and something every Christian should attempt to overcome. It is not surprising, then, that the second of Haman's sons to die would be named after self-pity.

Here are some very interesting secular quotes about self-pity that you might find useful:

> "I never saw a wild thing sorry for itself. A small bird will drop frozen dead from a bough without ever having felt sorry for itself."
>
> — D.H. Lawrence

> "Certainly the most destructive vice if you like, that a person can have. More than pride, which is supposedly the number one of the cardinal sins - is self-pity. Self-pity is the worst possible emotion anyone can have. And the most destructive. It is,

CHAPTER 2: THE SECOND SON - THE SAD SACK

to slightly paraphrase what Wilde said about hatred, and I think actually hatred's a subset of self-pity and not the other way around.

It destroys everything around it, except itself. Self-pity will destroy relationships, it'll destroy anything that's good, it will fulfill all the prophecies it makes and leave only itself. And it's so simple to imagine that one is hard done by, and that things are unfair, and that one is underappreciated, and that if only one had had a chance at this, only one had had a chance at that, things would have gone better, you would be happier if only this, that one is unlucky. All those things. And some of them may well even be true. But, to pity oneself as a result of them is to do oneself an enormous disservice.

I think it's one of things we find unattractive about the American culture, a culture which I find mostly, extremely attractive, and I like Americans and I love being in America. But, just occasionally there will be some example of the absolutely ravening self-pity that they are capable of, and you see it in their talk shows. It's an appalling spectacle, and it's

THE PSYCHOLOGY OF GOD: TEN SONS OF HAMAN

so self-destructive. I once almost wanted to publish a self-help book saying "How To Be Happy" by Stephen Fry: Guaranteed success. And people buy this huge book and its all blank pages, and the first page would just say - 'Stop Feeling Sorry For Yourself - And you will be happy.' Use the rest of the book to write down your interesting thoughts and drawings, and that's what the book would be, and it would be true. And it sounds like,'Oh that's so simple', because it's not simple to stop feeling sorry for yourself, it's bloody hard. Because we do feel sorry for ourselves, it's what Genesis is all about."

— Stephen Fry

"All depression has its roots in self-pity, and all self-pity is rooted in people taking themselves too seriously."

— Tom Robbins

"Satan exploits pain by making it the central focus of the man's (or woman's) thoughts and attitudes."

CHAPTER 2: THE SECOND SON - THE SAD SACK

— Erwin W. Lutzer, author of 'When You've Been Wronged: Moving From Bitterness to Forgiveness'

"Self-pity is a curse, which may lead to indignant behavior while a calm, non-competitive mind, achieves great feat. Competing with one self leads to blessing, while comparing oneself to others and then competing is a destructive path."

— Henrietta Newton Martin, Senior Legal Consultant & Author

CHAPTER 3

The Third Son - The Self-Made Man

The third son of Haman to be killed and hanged was named "Aspatha," which means "self-sufficient" or "assembled self." The meaning of this term, and why God would want us to avoid an excess of self-sufficiency is if we think we can do everything ourselves, we don't need Him. And nothing could be further from the truth.

The American value of "rugged individualism" or the "self-made man" (or woman) embodies the "assembled self," and although it is somewhat to be admired, it is also something to caution against, as one's ego tends to inflate that "we accomplished this by ourselves," instead of giving credit to God. It denies that we need Him and His guidance in all aspects of our lives.

John 5:5

> "I am the vine, ye are the branches: He that abideth in me, and I in him, the same bringeth forth much fruit: for without me ye can do nothing."

As you can see here, the Word of God teaches that we are nothing without Jesus Christ, and one tends to forget that all the blessings and successes we receive are through Him, not because of luck, or even our own doing, as much as our own drive and creativity might "get things done."

Colossians 1:17

And he is before all things, and by him all things consist.

Overly self-sufficient people also tend to deny the help of our brothers and sisters, and despite what we may think, other people are critical to our success. Without exception, other people have an impact on our work and well-being. When we turn people down because we are too self-sufficient, we rob the opportunity from friends and family to become more intimate with us, and to have bonds of sharing.

Being overly autonomous tends to make us self-focus, too. Our needs become the only things that matter, our work too important, our concerns focused inward instead of outward. It tends towards unilateral decisions, without considering those around us.

Philippians 2:4

Look not every man on his own things, but every man also on the things of others.

One needs a healthy balance of dependency and self-sufficiency in order to keep our lives truly in order, and to not isolate.

Here is a quote from *Psychology Today*, regarding an excess of independence:

CHAPTER 3: THE THIRD SON - THE SELF-MADE MAN

> "Researchers have found that people who avoid asking for help may suffer significant social and professional costs. They have a tendency to avoid seeking valuable help from educators or colleagues because involving others makes them feel needy. But by choosing to isolate in order to feel self-reliant, they may put themselves at risk of feeling unsupported or depressed."

In being like Aspatha, we tend to take on burdens that are too heavy, then complain that we have too much work to do. Mature Christians should know to let go of their ego when trying to accomplish something - and to allow others to help. That's why God often puts people in our path, exactly as we need them, and not surprisingly, they have the exact tools or experience we need to assist us. There are no coincidences. God blesses us with these things. Depending on others a little is a more efficient way to get things done as well.

Asking for help often doesn't result in direct, immediate, tangible help, but rather indirect help, as is fitting for God's involvement in our lives.

For instance, what we get instead of a helping hand, is good advice, and that is often ignored by people who are too independent. The suggestions that we get when we ask for help from others are the way in which God sometimes guides us, and dismissing that out of hand many times has perilous results, as most of us can attest. It's a blessing when others help us with their good counsel and advice, and something God puts in our path to help us. It also blesses others to be able to help us and being too independent removes that godly opportunity.

Hebrews 13:16

> *So that we may boldly say, The Lord is my helper, and I will not fear what man shall do unto me.*

Getting help from others is an opportunity to learn something new, too. It often creates new relationships, and can improve old friendships, improving intimacy and trust. All of these things are blessings from the Lord for which ideally we should always be thankful.

Self-sufficiency in the right amount is a positive thing; but nobody wants someone who is overly independent. Too much of a good thing is bad, so they say. In the case of the self-made man, bragging, which is something the Lord has told us not to do in His Word (so that none may boast), is generally the result:

Ephesians 2:8-10

> *For by grace are ye saved through faith; and that not of yourselves: it is the gift of God: Not of works, lest any man should boast. For we are his workmanship, created in Christ Jesus unto good works, which God hath before ordained that we should walk in them.*

CHAPTER 3: THE THIRD SON - THE SELF-MADE MAN

Have you ever seen someone who is bragging and overconfident in their abilities, be struck down into humility? It's not pretty but it happens, more often than not, to braggarts. Some would call it "Karma." I contend that Karma's other name is God. Mature Christians know to give others credit where credit is due, and God deserves a whale of credit in our lives, no matter who we are. Nobody is truly self-made; it takes support from those around us, and most notably, the providence of God.

CHAPTER 4

The Fourth Son - The Party Animal

"Poratha," the name of the fourth son of Haman, has two meanings; one, as someone spend-thrifty, or cheap, and another as self-indulgent. Although these two attributes almost seem at odds, if one realizes the reason for cheapness with others is to spend on oneself, one gets a grim picture of a selfish, self-indulgent personality that no one would like, and that symbolically God had executed, and then hanged. In fact, I get the feeling that this was the problem with Judas.

Much like self-pity, there's nothing 'redeeming,' again, in these meanings at all, concerning the name of "Poratha." There's no 'positive spin' on Hedonism or self-indulgence, as there is in some of the other sons' names, such as "independence. Self-gratification is self-indulgence, completely without regard to the welfare of others. It's unattractive to say the least. To say the most it's the most common attribute of pure evil. Without question, it is the opposite of what our Lord taught us about regarding others, that they are to be put first: Jesus asks us to serve others before ourselves. Selfish or self-indulgent behavior has no social benefits. Nor can this single personal psychological trait be utilized and rationalized in any positive way, because it goes beyond sheer survival of the person, by miles. The negatives outweigh the positives of self-indulgent individual behaviors in groups over time, even from a secular standpoint.

This is also another statement that we don't trust in God, when we grasp for things for ourselves. It says that we don't believe He's generous enough with us. Remember, we are not to worry about where our raiment will come from, or our food, because God royally clothes the lilies of the field and richly feeds the sparrow; how much more will He do for a child of God?

Matthew 10:28-31

> *And fear not them which kill the body, but are not able to kill the soul: but rather fear him which is able to destroy both soul and body in hell. Are not two sparrows sold for a farthing? and one of them shall not fall on the ground without your Father. But the very hairs of your head are all numbered. Fear ye not therefore, ye are of more value than many sparrows.*

Jesus serves as our living example and taught us to be giving to the poor, as He, Himself, deserved to live richly as a king, but instead, lived a Spartan life devoid of self-indulgence without even a place to lay His head. Jesus continues to teach through His Word, which tells us if we are asked for our shirt we are to give our cloak also (Luke 6:30).

CHAPTER 4: THE FOURTH SON - THE PARTY ANIMAL

In fact, it's not only just a negative personality attribute, self-indulgence is a mark of the end of times:

2 Timothy 3:1-5

> *This know also, that in the last days perilous times shall come. For men shall be lovers of their own selves, covetous, boasters, proud, blasphemers, disobedient to parents, unthankful, unholy, Without natural affection, trucebreakers, false accusers, incontinent, fierce, despisers of those that are good, Traitors, heady, highminded, lovers of pleasures more than lovers of God; Having a form of godliness, but denying the power thereof: from such turn away.*

"From such turn away!" - that's quite a statement. It gives no exceptions.

When we look through scripture we see a number of places where self-indulgence is spoken of directly, and how it's illustrated in Bible stories, where self-gratification and hedonism lead.

One story that might come to mind is the self-indulgent rich man, and Lazarus the beggar:

Luke 16:19-31

> *There was a certain rich man, which was clothed in purple and fine linen, and fared sumptuously every day: And there was a certain beggar named Lazarus, which was laid at his gate, full of sores, And desiring to*

be fed with the crumbs which fell from the rich man's table: moreover the dogs came and licked his sores. And it came to pass, that the beggar died, and was carried by the angels into Abraham's bosom: the rich man also died, and was buried; And in hell he lift up his eyes, being in torments, and seeth Abraham afar off, and Lazarus in his bosom. And he cried and said, Father Abraham, have mercy on me, and send Lazarus, that he may dip the tip of his finger in water, and cool my tongue; for I am tormented in this flame. But Abraham said, Son, remember that thou in thy lifetime receivedst thy good things, and likewise Lazarus evil things: but now he is comforted, and thou art tormented. And beside all this, between us and you there is a great gulf fixed: so that they which would pass from hence to you cannot; neither can they pass to us, that would come from thence. Then he said, I pray thee therefore, father, that thou wouldest send him to my father's house: For I have five brethren; that he may testify unto them, lest they also come into this place of torment. Abraham saith unto him, They have Moses and the prophets; let them hear them. And he said, Nay, father Abraham: but if one went unto them from the dead, they will repent. And he said unto him, If they hear not Moses and the prophets, neither will they be persuaded, though one rose from the dead.

So the Bible tells us that these types of people don't listen easily to the calls from history, or hell, to wake them up that the road they are on is a

CHAPTER 4: THE FOURTH SON - THE PARTY ANIMAL

dangerous one, as we see the last sentence of this passage:

> *And he said unto him, If they hear not Moses and the prophets, neither will they be persuaded, though one rose from the dead.*

There are so many examples, but we could start this examination of self-indulgent skinflints with Judas. Surely Judas, the traitorous apostle who mismanaged money, was probably one of the best examples of a cheapskate who was selfish; after all, he decried the expenditure on oil for Jesus' feet, but, at the same time, took 30 pieces of silver for himself from the Pharisees, the enemies of God, for turning in his best friend, brother, and Creator, Jesus Himself. He even kissed Jesus to point him out in the crowd. It turns the stomach of any true believer.

But there are more examples, such as Ananias and Sapphira. These were people who actually robbed from the church itself by lying about the amount they sold some land for. These lying, selfish, money-grubbers were struck dead by God. And people were afraid when they heard these words, and who can blame them! There are lots of self-indulgent people who cheat money from the church for their own pleasure. I wouldn't want to be standing in their shoes when Jesus returns.

Another story that illustrates God's hatred for selfishness and cheapness with others, from 1 Samuel 25, is of a cheapskate who was Abigail's husband, whose name 'Nabal' actually meant "fool." He insulted some of David's men who were crossing his field one day. King David heard about it and it angered him, so he set out with 400 men to Nabal's land, possibly to kill Nabal and his family for such an act.

Abigail, one of the only women in scripture described as "beautiful," and being Nabal's wife, she was concerned for her household. She realized the error that Nabal had made in not being hospitable to David's men. She thus greeted the angry King David and his men with loaves of bread, wine, dressed sheep, roasted grains, and cakes. She apologized for her foolish, ungrateful husband. David accepted Abigail's apology and spared her household, but God did not spare Nabal. The next morning, after Nabal had sobered up, Abagail told him what had transpired while he was drunk. His heart failed, he died soon after, and David took Abigail as his wife.

Examples of self-indulgent behavior are throughout the Bible; there's the account of the dances of seven veils that the daughter of Herodias did for the King celebrating his birthday; there's the selfishness and self-indulgence of Jezebel and her King Ahab, robbing Naboth's land by having him falsely accused and executed. No wonder God allowed her to be killed and fed to dogs. There is plenty to think about for people who understand these scriptures.

The self-indulgent prodigal son is another great example. He squandered everything on loose living

CHAPTER 4: THE FOURTH SON - THE PARTY ANIMAL

before becoming impoverished. And this concept of "loose living leads to a lack of discipline" would be supported elsewhere in scripture, for instance, in Proverbs it tells us that those who love lush living will never become wealthy:

Proverbs 21:17

> *The robbery of the wicked shall destroy them; because they refuse to do judgment.*

The futile and shallow nature of self-indulgence is also portrayed as a form of death:

1 Timothy 5:6

> *But she that liveth in pleasure is dead while she liveth.*

The Lord expresses to us His view about storing up "treasures on the earth" instead of treasures in heaven, citing the futile and ephemeral nature of earthly self-indulgence:

Luke 12:18-21

> *And he said, This will I do: I will pull down my barns, and build greater; and there will I bestow all my fruits and my goods. And I will say to my soul, Soul, thou hast much goods laid up for many years; take thine ease, eat, drink, and be merry. But God said unto him, Thou fool, this night thy soul shall be required of thee: then whose shall those things be, which thou hast provided? So is he that layeth up treasure for himself, and is not rich toward God.*

In addressing the Pharisees, Jesus chastised them for their self-indulgence and corruption:

Matthew 23:25

> *Woe unto you, scribes and Pharisees, hypocrites! for ye make clean the outside of the cup and of the platter, but within they are full of extortion and excess.*

In the description of how the holy should live, we see references to "lush living" and self-indulgence:

Ephesians 4:17-32

> *This I say therefore, and testify in the Lord, that ye henceforth walk not as other Gentiles walk, in the vanity of their mind, Having the understanding darkened, being alienated from the life of God through the ignorance that is in them, because of the blindness of their heart: Who being past feeling have given themselves over unto lasciviousness, to work all uncleanness with greediness. But ye have not so learned Christ; If so be that ye have heard him, and have been taught by him, as the truth is in Jesus: That ye put off concerning the former conversation the old man, which is corrupt according to the deceitful lusts; And be renewed in the spirit of your mind; And that ye put on the new man, which after God is created in righteousness and true holiness. Wherefore putting away lying, speak every man truth with his neighbour: for we are members one of another. Be ye angry, and sin not: let not*

CHAPTER 4: THE FOURTH SON - THE PARTY ANIMAL

the sun go down upon your wrath: Neither give place to the devil. Let him that stole steal no more: but rather let him labour, working with his hands the thing which is good, that he may have to give to him that needeth. Let no corrupt communication proceed out of your mouth, but that which is good to the use of edifying, that it may minister grace unto the hearers. And grieve not the holy Spirit of God, whereby ye are sealed unto the day of redemption. Let all bitterness, and wrath, and anger, and clamour, and evil speaking, be put away from you, with all malice: And be ye kind one to another, tenderhearted, forgiving one another, even as God for Christ's sake hath forgiven you.

In fact, we are not even to associate with these types of self-indulgent people:

Proverbs 23:20

Be not among winebibbers; among riotous eaters of flesh:

There are a lot more examples throughout the Bible of people who are self-indulgent, hedonistic, lovers of the flesh, or serving the flesh. One example is the daughter of Herodias, at the King's birthday party. She did the dance of the seven veils that led to the death of John the Baptist.

Pharaoh was a rich hedonist, stubborn and prideful, with his own magicians, and refused to bend his knees to God. This is a profile that we see of many people today. In the Bible, there's the story of "The Rich Man." The man had come to Jesus asking what he needed to do to be saved. He explained that he already adhered to the ten commandments but wanted to know what else he might have to do to be saved. Jesus told him to give up his belongings. Jesus knew from the man's heart that this was what he needed. So Jesus said it - give it all up - all his riches. Because the Rich Man couldn't give away what he had, he went away sad.

Lot's wife is another really great example of the dangers of a hedonistic life. She missed the corruption and fleshly self-indulgences of Sodom. So she looked back when the Lord had expressly told Lot and her not to do so. So she was turned to a pillar of salt.

The Whore of Babylon is described as a woman who drank the wine of the blood of the saints, and lived deliciously, and would not be a widow, and would fornicate with the kings of the earth. Look at this description; it is vile in the eyes of the Lord.

Colossians 2:20-23

> *Wherefore if ye be dead with Christ from the rudiments of the world, why, as though living in the world, are ye subject to ordinances, (Touch not; taste not; handle not; Which all are to perish with the using;) after the commandments and doctrines of men? Which things have indeed a shew of wisdom in will worship, and humility, and neglecting*

CHAPTER 4: THE FOURTH SON - THE PARTY ANIMAL

of the body; not in any honour to the satisfying of the flesh.

Here's another point about today's world and self-indulgence; the Western World has been providing pornography globally, as well as aborting millions upon millions of babies for the convenience of casual sex. Our society now propagates the acceptance of homosexuality around the world, as well as pedophilia and adultery. America and Europe have become Sodom and Gomorrah, to a magnitude that the stench is reaching the nostrils of Our Father in Heaven. He will not ignore it.

CHAPTER 5

The Fifth Son - The Snowflake

Mark 12:30 (KJV)

*And thou shalt love the Lord thy God with all thy heart, and with all thy soul, and with all thy mind, **and with all thy strength:** this is the first commandment.*

The fifth son of Haman to perish twice is "Adalia," which means "weak self."

There has been some debate whether or not this meaning is translated to "humble self." Humility is a desirable quality in people, so it's hard to imagine that humbleness would be something the Lord wouldn't desire in His children's array of personality traits. But there is a relationship between a false humbleness, and weakness. It is said that Haman went around bragging about how humble he was, and this helps illustrate one of those relationships. Jesus fills us with strength, as the Word of God teaches in several places. We will discuss how the weakness of the human spirit, depends upon God ultimately for its strength.

2 Corinthians 12:9

And he said unto me, My grace is sufficient for thee: for my strength is made perfect in

> *weakness. Most gladly therefore will I rather glory in my infirmities, that the power of Christ may rest upon me.*

One of the examples of humility as weakness in the Bible is when people have told the Lord that they aren't strong enough to do as He asks of them. A prime example is Moses.

The Lord asked Moses to go to the Egyptians and speak to them. In fact, He had asked him more than once, and Moses kept offering excuses. At first, Moses said he didn't know the Name of God. At the second request, Moses fell upon a false humility to avoid doing as God asked:

Exodus 4:10

> *And Moses said unto the LORD, O my Lord, I am not eloquent, neither heretofore, nor since thou hast spoken unto thy servant: but I am slow of speech, and of a slow tongue.*

This is tantamount to saying, "Oh Lord, you have created me too weak," a "humble" stance, but he forgot who made us, and that He can bestow on us strength anytime He wants.

So God answered Moses this way:

Exodus 4:11-12

> *And the LORD said unto him, Who hath made man's mouth? or who maketh the dumb, or deaf, or the seeing, or the blind? have not I the LORD? Now therefore go, and*

CHAPTER 5: THE FIFTH SON - THE SNOWFLAKE

> *I will be with thy mouth, and teach thee what thou shalt say.*

The anger of the Lord burned against Moses because of his clinging to his weakness, in unwarranted humility.

Demonstrating this is in the truth found in Philippians 4:13 which states: *"I can do all things through Christ which strengtheneth me."*

He also shows us the truth in Romans 8:26, as we read:

Romans 8:26

> *Likewise the Spirit also helpeth our infirmities: for we know not what we should pray for as we ought: but the Spirit itself maketh intercession for us with groanings which cannot be uttered.*

This asserts that even when we are totally confused, and don't know how to pray or what to pray for, the Holy Spirit helps us, and strengthens us, and guides us.

Beyond "humble self," the "weak self" describing the weakness of human spirit is also something God wants us to banish from our inner selves because we are created in His image. He provides us with strength, if only we will ask. Jesus says (James 4:2), *"ye have not, because ye ask not."*

2 Corinthians 12:9-10

And he said unto me, My grace is sufficient for thee: for my strength is made perfect in weakness. Most gladly therefore will I rather glory in my infirmities, that the power of Christ may rest upon me. Therefore I take pleasure in infirmities, in reproaches, in necessities, in persecutions, in distresses for Christ's sake: for when I am weak, then am I strong.

In fact, God promises strength of all kinds to us, in our hour of need, even as it pertains to the physical:

Isaiah 40:29-31

He giveth power to the faint; and to them that have no might he increaseth strength. Even the youths shall faint and be weary, and the young men shall utterly fall: But they that wait upon the LORD shall renew their strength; they shall mount up with wings as eagles; they shall run, and not be weary; and they shall walk, and not faint.

It is clear that this is a paradox, but understandable through scripture - that God wants us to acknowledge our weakness, so He can convert it to strength. We cannot feign humility in order to cling to our weaknesses because He knows our hearts.

God never wants us to be weak, and afraid, even in the face of natural disaster, which is clear in Matthew 8:26:

CHAPTER 5: THE FIFTH SON - THE SNOWFLAKE

Matthew 8:24-26

> *And, behold, there arose a great tempest in the sea, insomuch that the ship was covered with the waves: but he was asleep. And his disciples came to him, and awoke him, saying, Lord, save us: we perish. And he saith unto them, Why are ye fearful, O ye of little faith? Then he arose, and rebuked the winds and the sea; and there was a great calm.*

Look at how the Lord blessed David for his righteous, bold strength against the mighty Goliath. This is strength in the Lord. Imagine the level of trust David had as he shouted out:

1 Samuel 17:45-46

> *Then said David to the Philistine, Thou comest to me with a sword, and with a spear, and with a shield: but I come to thee in the name of the LORD of hosts, the God of the armies of Israel, whom thou hast defied. This day will the LORD deliver thee into mine hand; and I will smite thee, and take thine head from thee; and I will give the carcases of the host of the Philistines this day unto the fowls of the air, and to the wild beasts of the earth; that all the earth may know that there is a God in Israel.*

God said David was *"a man after His own heart"* (1 Samuel 13:14).

David believed the Lord. And the Lord teaches us to trust Him, and, as He is the Word made flesh, we know He keeps His promises. The scriptures say:

Isaiah 41:10

Fear thou not; for I am with thee: be not dismayed; for I am thy God: I will strengthen thee; yea, I will help thee; yea, I will uphold thee with the right hand of my righteousness.

Philippians 4:13

I can do all things through Christ which strengtheneth me.

2 Timothy 1:7

For God hath not given us the spirit of fear; but of power, and of love, and of a sound mind.

2 Thessalonians 3:3

But the Lord is faithful, who shall stablish you, and keep you from evil.

Psalm 18:1-2 (See 2 Sam 22:2)

"I will love thee, O Lord, my strength. The Lord is my rock, and my fortress, and my deliverer; my God, my strength, in whom I will trust; my buckler, and the horn of my salvation, and my high tower.

Psalm 59:16

But I will sing of thy power; yea, I will sing aloud of thy mercy in the morning: for thou

CHAPTER 5: THE FIFTH SON - THE SNOWFLAKE

hast been my defence and refuge in the day of my trouble.

Ephesians 6:10

Finally, my brethren, be strong in the Lord, and in the power of his might.

CHAPTER 6

The Sixth Son - The Bully

Genesis 32:24-30

> *And Jacob was left alone; and there wrestled a man with him until the breaking of the day. And when he saw that he prevailed not against him, he touched the hollow of his thigh; and the hollow of Jacob's thigh was out of joint, as he wrestled with him. And he said, Let me go, for the day breaketh. And he said, I will not let thee go, except thou bless me. And he said unto him, What is thy name? And he said, Jacob. And he said, Thy name shall be called no more Jacob, but Israel: for as a prince hast thou power with God and with men, and hast prevailed. And Jacob asked him, and said, Tell me, I pray thee, thy name. And he said, Wherefore is it that thou dost ask after my name? And he blessed him there. And Jacob called the name of the place Peniel: for I have seen God face to face, and my life is preserved.*

The sixth son of Haman to perish is "Aridatha." It has a meaning that might be confusing at first when we consider that both weak, strong, and "bold" terms are translated when we examine the various names of Haman's sons. Its primary meaning is "the strong self," or, "self-assertive." It might be akin to 'overbearing,' but I believe its meaning goes even deeper.

The discussion in the previous chapter was about God's directive not to be too weak, and to know we have strength in Him. The very next name means to be strong, and yet it's also killed and hung as a son of Haman. So we might wonder why God wouldn't want us to be too strong.

Nobody likes bullying, and a self-assertive person is seen as a bully when aggressiveness gets out of control. In fact, good leadership is linked in psychological studies to the right amount of self-assertive behavior. But we know that God wishes us to be strong in general, that we are to pray for strength, but as we examine this particular name, we see that the deeper meaning is to be strong against the Lord, or, our "assertive self," or, going our "own way"...without Him.

Wrestling with God, like Jacob did, is what I see as being a great analogy to this teaching. Being 'self-assertive' means to depart from what God has designed for our lives, directly against what He has told us to do. In the Word of God we see that disobedience often has dire consequences. This began with Adam and Eve in the garden, who went against what God had told them not to do.

There are quite a few stories in biblical scripture that illuminate the folly of not listening to the Lord, and going our own way, against His ways. Two men who come immediately to mind are Jonah and Lot. Jonah and Lot both loved God, but also were weak and disobedient, which illustrates how God deals with "self-assertive" people who go against His will.

CHAPTER 6: THE SIXTH SON - THE BULLY

Jonah had been asked by the Lord specifically to go to Nineveh to preach, and Jonah didn't want to, because they were enemies of his, so, he didn't listen to God. He had his own ideas about things. He was willing to let his enemies die in their sins. That isn't what God had in mind. Here's what happened:

Jonah 1:1-4

> *Now the word of the LORD came unto Jonah the son of Amittai, saying, Arise, go to Nineveh, that great city, and cry against it; for their wickedness is come up before me. But Jonah rose up to flee unto Tarshish from the presence of the LORD, and went down to Joppa; and he found a ship going to Tarshish: so he paid the fare thereof, and went down into it, to go with them unto Tarshish from the presence of the LORD. But the LORD sent out a great wind into the sea, and there was a mighty tempest in the sea, so that the ship was like to be broken.*

The Lord hurled a great wind on the sea and there was a great storm on the sea so that the ship was about to break up.

You would think that right off the bat, Jonah would see that the Lord wasn't pleased. But instead, the Bible says, he went to sleep aboard the ship!

Being self-assertive themselves, the men on the ship had tried everything, including throwing everything overboard to lighten the load of the ship. But of course, nothing worked. Here the story continues in scripture:

Jonah 1:5-7

> *Then the sailors became afraid and every man cried to his god, and they threw the cargo which was in the ship into the sea to lighten it for them. But Jonah had gone below into the hold of the ship, lain down and fallen sound asleep. So the captain approached him and said, "How is it that you are sleeping? Get up, call on your god. Perhaps your god will be concerned about us so that we will not perish." Each man said to his mate, "Come, let us cast lots so we may learn on whose account this calamity has struck us." So they cast lots and the lot fell on Jonah.*

Evidently, Jonah hadn't figured on God objecting so much to his plans, and it shows that his "strong self" had taken over, steering his life in a different direction than the Lord had requested of him. Point in fact, when Jonah realized it was the Lord that was causing the great storm, he told the men to throw him into the sea, to appease the Lord. The men were unwilling to do so. They were unwilling to throw a man into the sea because, it appears, they didn't believe in "Jonah's god," as we saw them "crying to the gods" of their own. Eventually, Jonah told them. He said to them:

CHAPTER 6: THE SIXTH SON - THE BULLY

Jonah 1:12

And he said unto them, Take me up, and cast me forth into the sea; so shall the sea be calm unto you: for I know that for my sake this great tempest is upon you.

Jonah had earlier explained that he was a Hebrew and explained who God was (maker of sea and dry land). Really, this was a golden opportunity for Jonah to witness for "his God," as the sailors were praying to their own gods and getting no answers. So naturally, what did they do? Again, going to their own strength, they attempted to row harder than ever, to get to land on their own steam. But of course, things only got worse, and they couldn't overpower God.

Jonah 1:13

Nevertheless the men rowed hard to bring it to the land; but they could not: for the sea wrought, and was tempestuous against them.

Finally, with their own "self-assertive" plan failing, they finally called upon the Lord... Jonah's "Hebrew God", as Jonah had witnessed to them, and now they changed their strategy:

Jonah 1:14-16

Wherefore they cried unto the LORD, and said, We beseech thee, O LORD, we beseech thee, let us not perish for this man's life, and lay not upon us innocent blood: for thou, O LORD, hast done as it pleased thee.

> *So they took up Jonah, and cast him forth into the sea: and the sea ceased from her raging. Then the men feared the LORD exceedingly, and offered a sacrifice unto the LORD, and made vows.*

Now they became believers, it seems, for they prayed to the God of the Israelites. They subjugated their own self-assertive behavior to the will of the Lord, and their prayers were answered. After throwing Jonah into the sea, God placed Jonah in the belly of the great fish (called a whale in Matthew 12:40):

Jonah 1:17

> *Now the LORD had prepared a great fish to swallow up Jonah. And Jonah was in the belly of the fish three days and three nights.*

In the belly of the fish, Jonah calls out to the Lord, and prays to Him. He cries out that the Lord is his salvation. This is the lesson that God wanted Jonah to learn. Because of this, the fish then vomits Jonah up.

Subsequently, after Jonah is freed from the great fish's belly, God asks him again to go to Nineveh and preach. This time, of course, no longer being self-assertive, Jonah listens and does as the Lord asked of him. Wise choice!

It's a good lesson for Jonah, and for anyone who reads and understands this story, to learn vicariously, not to reject God's plans for us as Christians. Jonah's mission to Nineveh was very

CHAPTER 6: THE SIXTH SON - THE BULLY

successful. Instead of destroying that city, their great repentance kept them from being destroyed.

A second story that comes to mind when considering "self-assertiveness," and the calamity it can bring, is the story of Lot and his wife.

Lot knew of the corruption of Sodom, and yet, instead of staying far away from it, he pitched his tent right "towards Sodom," or, "on the edge" of Sodom. This was quite a self-assertive thing to do because he knew it to be evil. It is never wise, keeping one foot so near evil.

Genesis 13:10-13

> *And Lot lifted up his eyes, and beheld all the plain of Jordan, that it was well watered every where, before the LORD destroyed Sodom and Gomorrah, even as the garden of the LORD, like the land of Egypt, as thou comest unto Zoar. Then Lot chose him all the plain of Jordan; and Lot journeyed east: and they separated themselves the one from the other. Abram dwelled in the land of Canaan, and Lot dwelled in the cities of the plain, and pitched his tent toward Sodom. But the men of Sodom were wicked and sinners before the LORD exceedingly.*

Abram, who separated from Lot, was then promised blessings from the Lord. Lot was not. However, Lot was considered a righteous man by the Lord, and His sympathy and protection stayed with him, as we shall see.

It seems that although Lot was "self-assertive" and not doing what God wanted for him, the Lord was still watching out for him. In fact, in Genesis 19, when we see Lot is approached by the "strangers" (angels), he is actually sitting at Sodom's gate:

Genesis 19:1

> *And there came two angels to Sodom at even; and Lot sat in the gate of Sodom: and Lot seeing them rose up to meet them; and he bowed himself with his face toward the ground;*

Yet God, somehow, regarded Lot as a "righteous man" but evidently on the wrong path. In the story told in Genesis 19, after Lot insists the angels come to his house, and he feeds them, before they can go to bed that night the people of Sodom surround the house. They try to break down the door, and threaten him, because they want to have sex with the "strangers."

It is shocking to modern sensibilities to see Lot offered up his virginal daughters to the crowd in order to appease the mob, and in order to protect the "men" sheltered in Lot's house. Lot's strategy doesn't work, so the angels strike the Sodomites blind. They wind up groping the floor, and unable to attack the people inside Lot's house.

The angels then warn Lot that they will destroy the city. They tell him to flee to the hills. Even then, Lot tells them he is afraid of what might befall him

CHAPTER 6: THE SIXTH SON - THE BULLY

in the hills. He insists that he wants to go to the city of Zoar. The two angels sent from the Lord are amazingly compassionate toward Lot, because when he lingers there after their warning, the angels then take Lot by the hand, and lead him away from there. They postpone the destruction of Sodom until Lot arrives in Zoar, safely away.

As most mature Christians know, the angels tell Lot and his family not to look back upon the city as they are leaving, or they will be killed. Of course, we also know the self-assertive wife of Lot, who apparently enjoyed the evil of Sodom, couldn't resist looking back just once. Thus she was turned into a pillar of salt:

Genesis 19:23-26

> *The sun was risen upon the earth when Lot entered into Zoar. Then the LORD rained upon Sodom and upon Gomorrah brimstone and fire from the LORD out of heaven; And he overthrew those cities, and all the plain, and all the inhabitants of the cities, and that which grew upon the ground. But his wife looked back from behind him, and she became a pillar of salt.*

It is interesting to note that Lot was spared, possibly because of Abraham, further showing the truth of the Word of God which states that because of our faith, our relatives and family are often blessed:

THE PSYCHOLOGY OF GOD: TEN SONS OF HAMAN

Genesis 19:27-29

> *And Abraham gat up early in the morning to the place where he stood before the LORD: And he looked toward Sodom and Gomorrah, and toward all the land of the plain, and beheld, and, lo, the smoke of the country went up as the smoke of a furnace. And it came to pass, when God destroyed the cities of the plain, that God remembered Abraham, and sent Lot out of the midst of the overthrow, when he overthrew the cities in the which Lot dwelt.*

Truly our Lord is compassionate, even towards the believers who are sometimes foolish and self-assertive. He is faithful towards all who love Him. These two stories are testimony to that fact. If you search the scriptures further, you will find even more stories, such as the story of Cain and Abel, two of the children of Adam and Eve.

Cain was also self-assertive. He didn't worship as God had asked. For his sacrifice he brought vegetables, that didn't require real sacrifice (the killing of animals, and blood). He wound up killing his brother Abel out of jealousy when God's favor wasn't upon him.

How do these biblical examples apply to us as believers? God wants the "self-assertive" behavior in us, the "bold self" that is against the Lord, to die, as witnessed by the fact that it's one of the sons. Every single one of the deaths of the sons of Haman points to a negative attribute of mankind

CHAPTER 6: THE SIXTH SON - THE BULLY

hidden within the name of each one. The Lord clearly wants to be everything to us, and for us to follow Him without question. That is directly said by the Lord Jesus, in John 20:29.

John 20:29

Jesus saith unto him, Thomas, because thou hast seen me, thou hast believed: blessed are they that have not seen, and yet have believed.

Following what the Lord wants for us isn't always easy, and sometimes we cannot "see" why things are happening the way they are. Some people will give up, and instead fall upon the easy, broad road when faced with the difficulty of climbing the narrow road. Sometimes following what the Lord asks of us can lead to all kinds of mocking, persecution, discomfort, social rejection, and even danger or peril. Regardless, the Lord is always with us, and will protect us. He promises us this, as followers. Trusting in that isn't easy, but over time, we learn that it's the best way to go because He is so faithful to His Word.

The narrow road, although rocky and treacherous, and full of the effort of ever climbing upward through great struggles, leads to rewards in heaven.

THE PSYCHOLOGY OF GOD: TEN SONS OF HAMAN

CHAPTER 7

The Seventh Son - The Narcissist

The name of the seventh son of Haman to be killed and hung is easily seen as an old problem with humans. "Parmashta," the name of the seventh son means "preeminent self" or "self-ambition," a problem beginning with Satan, and going on through Cain and the rest of humanity.

It's clear that the meaning of this name suggests to be "ambitious for oneself" is, by definition, to always think of oneself first, the "self being pre-eminent" before all things, including God. Being a selfish person, putting oneself first in the extreme, is clinically described as narcissism. Jesus taught us the opposite; to think of others first, before ourselves. There are a number of "disorders" that make us full of self-ambition, opportunism, narcissism, and selfishness, all of which are described in the lexicon of the DSM-5 ("Diagnostic and Statistical of Mental Disorders" published by the American Psychiatric Association, the industry manual from which doctors and therapists get the 'definition' of 'disorders') with words such as, "oppositional defiant personality," "borderline personality," "narcissistic personality," etc.

The Bible is rife with examples of self-ambition, without using this lexicon, where people put themselves ahead of others. It never mentions "mental illness" in these stories because it isn't a matter of disease of the mind, but of disease of the spirit. The Psychology industry does not talk about evil or the human spirit. It talks about disorder, disease, and malfunction. It's rather like a heart surgeon looking into the brain for the problem of cardiac infarction.

The Bible also gives examples where someone put themselves before another, as the Word teaches that the greatest gift is for one friend to die for another. Jesus is the ultimate example of this, as He put down His life to save you and me.

Who were Ananias and Sapphira thinking of when they hatched their evil plan to lie to the church and keep money for themselves? They weren't thinking of God or their brothers or sisters in the church.

Acts 5:5-11 (KJV)

> *And Ananias hearing these words fell down, and gave up the ghost: and great fear came on all them that heard these things. And the young men arose, wound him up, and carried him out, and buried him. And it was about the space of three hours after, when his wife, not knowing what was done, came in. And Peter answered unto her, Tell me whether ye sold the land for so much? And she said, Yea, for so much. Then Peter said*

CHAPTER 7: THE SEVENTH SON - THE NARCISSIST

> *unto her, How is it that ye have agreed together to tempt the Spirit of the Lord? behold, the feet of them which have buried thy husband are at the door, and shall carry thee out. Then fell she down straightway at his feet, and yielded up the ghost: and the young men came in, and found her dead, and, carrying her forth, buried her by her husband. And great fear came upon all the church, and upon as many as heard these things.*

Self-ambition is a very natural trait that every human being has been guilty of, to some degree, in our lives. So, self-ambition is one of the most illustrated aspects of personality in the whole of scripture. The self-ambitions of Ananias and Sapphira are excellent models to show the results of such ambitions, driven by greed and carnal lusts.

We see so many people going after their own ambitions, some in a positive light, some in a negative. An example of negative and carnal ambitions is Jezebel and her King Ahab's desire to own a particular piece of property. Jezebel's plot led to the death of the property owner, Naboth. The ambition of Jezebel led to braking multiple commandments (do not covet, steal, murder). Ultimately, that brought about the gruesome end of Jezebel.

1 Kings 21:17-24

> *And the word of the LORD came to Elijah the Tishbite, saying, Arise, go down to meet Ahab king of Israel, which is in Samaria:*

behold, he is in the vineyard of Naboth, whither he is gone down to possess it. And thou shalt speak unto him, saying, Thus saith the LORD, Hast thou killed, and also taken possession? And thou shalt speak unto him, saying, Thus saith the LORD, In the place where dogs licked the blood of Naboth shall dogs lick thy blood, even thine. And Ahab said to Elijah, Hast thou found me, O mine enemy? And he answered, I have found thee: because thou hast sold thyself to work evil in the sight of the LORD. Behold, I will bring evil upon thee, and will take away thy posterity, and will cut off from Ahab him that pisseth against the wall, and him that is shut up and left in Israel, And will make thine house like the house of Jeroboam the son of Nebat, and like the house of Baasha the son of Ahijah, for the provocation wherewith thou hast provoked me to anger, and made Israel to sin. And of Jezebel also spake the LORD, saying, The dogs shall eat Jezebel by the wall of Jezreel. Him that dieth of Ahab in the city the dogs shall eat; and him that dieth in the field shall the fowls of the air eat.

But we also see self-ambition in Jacob and Esau. Esau's ambition to have the blessings of his father was circumvented by the ambitions of his mother and Jacob. And this wasn't something punished by God. This astounds some people, but when we look at the self-ambition of Esau, we see he married two Hittite women that vexed his mother. These women clearly were not good or godly, or Rachel would have loved them. *"If Jacob take a wife of the daughters of Heth, . . .what good*

CHAPTER 7: THE SEVENTH SON - THE NARCISSIST

shall my life do to me?" is quite a desperate statement. Fortunately, Jacob listened to his parents and married a woman from Canaan. Jacob was an obedient son. Esau was a man with poor decision-making from what we see. He failed to honor is father and mother in favor of his own ambition.

The self-ambition of Eve is probably the most classic of all. Her ambition to be "like God" was something that the snake knew he could play upon to get her to believe God is a liar. And she did. Her self-ambition came crashing down immediately, and her recompense was ejection from the garden.

The ambition of Judas to get the silver coins offered for the betrayal of Jesus also came crashing down immediately, and he later threw the money back at the Pharisees. This demonstrates that he knew his grave error as he went to hang himself.

On the other hand, the ambition of Jabez wasn't thwarted. Jabez's prayer is very famous and is different from other prayers. Why? Because he specifically asks God to help his ambitions, while praying that those ambitions do not lead to the harm of anyone else. That is very significant. It's a clear message that the ambitions of men are fine with God, approved by Him, as long as we do not hurt other people in doing so.

We hear of men in the Bible who were generous to others. In fact in Jeremiah 29:11, we see that God has great plans for us; that He wants us to prosper! We see that He has no plans to harm us; that the Lord wants us to succeed. By doing that, we can give to the poor, and prosper ourselves, which is the glory of God. Jesus said the poor would always be among us, and hence the opportunity to give is always with us.

Jeremiah 29:11

> *For I know the thoughts that I think toward you, saith the LORD, thoughts of peace, and not of evil, to give you an expected end.*

The Bible teaches money in itself is not evil; it is the "love of money" that is the root of all evil; so our success must be tied to helping the poor, if we do succeed financially.

Hebrews 13:16

> *But to do good and to communicate forget not: for with such sacrifices God is well pleased.*

Proverbs 19:17

> *He that hath pity upon the poor lendeth unto the LORD; and that which he hath given will he pay him again.*

Acts 20:35

> *I have shewed you all things, how that so labouring ye ought to support the weak, and to remember the words of the Lord Jesus, how he said, It is more blessed to give than to receive.*

CHAPTER 7: THE SEVENTH SON - THE NARCISSIST

1 John 3:17

But whoso hath this world's good, and seeth his brother have need, and shutteth up his bowels of compassion from him, how dwelleth the love of God in him?

Matthew 6:1-4

Take heed that ye do not your alms before men, to be seen of them: otherwise ye have no reward of your Father which is in heaven. Therefore when thou doest thine alms, do not sound a trumpet before thee, as the hypocrites do in the synagogues and in the streets, that they may have glory of men. Verily I say unto you, They have their reward. But when thou doest alms, let not thy left hand know what thy right hand doeth: That thine alms may be in secret: and thy Father which seeth in secret himself shall reward thee openly.

Deuteronomy 15:7-11

If there be among you a poor man of one of thy brethren within any of thy gates in thy land which the LORD thy God giveth thee, thou shalt not harden thine heart, nor shut thine hand from thy poor brother: But thou shalt open thine hand wide unto him, and shalt surely lend him sufficient for his need, in that which he wanteth. Beware that there be not a thought in thy wicked heart, saying, The seventh year, the year of release, is at hand; and thine eye be evil against thy poor brother, and thou givest him nought; and he

> cry unto the LORD against thee, and it be sin unto thee. Thou shalt surely give him, and thine heart shall not be grieved when thou givest unto him: because that for this thing the LORD thy God shall bless thee in all thy works, and in all that thou puttest thine hand unto. For the poor shall never cease out of the land: therefore I command thee, saying, Thou shalt open thine hand wide unto thy brother, to thy poor, and to thy needy, in thy land.

Matthew 5:42

> Give to him that asketh thee, and from him that would borrow of thee turn not thou away.

There are plenty more statements like these, if you search for them. That's because God tells us repeatedly that we must share our successes, from the fruits of those healthy ambitions, with others who are less fortunate.

CHAPTER 8

The Eighth Son - The Over-Confident One

The eighth son to die and be hanged is called "Arisai" and means "bold self" or "I am bold." Under what conditions does God want boldness to die?

Being bold in our faith is wonderful. The Bible speaks about this in glowing terms. However, there's a point at which boldness goes overboard. Without sufficient strength or knowledge to back us up, our boldness can turn into overconfidence. Overly bold people are humbled or punished by God as can be seen by the boldness of those who built the Tower of Babel.

Genesis 11:4

> *And they said, Go to, let us build us a city and a tower, whose top may reach unto heaven; and let us make us a name, lest we be scattered abroad upon the face of the whole earth.*

Genesis 11:8-9

> *So the LORD scattered them abroad from thence upon the face of all the earth: and they left off to build the city. Therefore is the name of it called Babel; because the LORD did there confound the language of all the*

> *earth: and from thence did the LORD scatter them abroad upon the face of all the earth.*

We can easily see that overconfidence isn't a human attribute that our Father likes, in any way, and you can find examples throughout the Bible, of this concept. The Bible sums it up, so:

1 Corinthians 1:27

> *But God hath chosen the foolish things of the world to confound the wise; and God hath chosen the weak things of the world to confound the things which are mighty;*

Like most of these Haman-Son attributes, there's a "flip side" that is positive - boldness is something the Word encourages. Here are some examples of how righteous boldness is something that God cultivates in His people.

Proverbs 28:1

> *The wicked flee when no man pursueth: but the righteous are bold as a lion.*

2 Corinthians 3:11-12

> *For if that which is done away was glorious, much more that which remaineth is glorious. Seeing then that we have such hope, we use great plainness of speech:*

Hebrews 4:16

> *Let us therefore come boldly unto the throne of grace, that we may obtain mercy, and find grace to help in time of need.*

CHAPTER 8: THE EIGHTH SON - THE OVER-CONFIDENT ONE

Psalm 138: 3

In the day when I cried thou answeredst me, and strengthenedst me with strength in my soul.

2 Corinthians 4:8-10

We are troubled on every side, yet not distressed; we are perplexed, but not in despair; Persecuted, but not forsaken; cast down, but not destroyed; Always bearing about in the body the dying of the Lord Jesus, that the life also of Jesus might be made manifest in our body.

When I think of an example of religious boldness, I think of when David had to slay the giant, Goliath. He not only slew him, but did so with religious boldness. Boldness in relying upon God.

1 Samuel 17:45-50

Then said David to the Philistine, Thou comest to me with a sword, and with a spear, and with a shield: but I come to thee in the name of the Lord of hosts, the God of the armies of Israel, whom thou hast defied. This day will the Lord deliver thee into mine hand; and I will smite thee, and take thine head from thee; and I will give the carcasses of the host of the Philistines this day unto the fowls of the air, and to the wild beasts of the earth; that all the earth may know that there is a God in Israel. And all this assembly shall know that the Lord saveth not with sword and spear: for the battle is the Lord's, and he

> *will give you into our hands. And it came to pass, when the Philistine arose, and came, and drew nigh to meet David, that David hastened, and ran toward the army to meet the Philistine. And David put his hand in his bag, and took thence a stone, and slang it, and smote the Philistine in his forehead, that the stone sunk into his forehead; and he fell upon his face to the earth. So David prevailed over the Philistine with a sling and with a stone, and smote the Philistine, and slew him; but there was no sword in the hand of David.*

David, without a sword, had the sheer boldness to kill Goliath. Righteous boldness because he knew and served his Lord.

But boldness can also be negative when we are without God. Without our Lord to guide us, our boldness isn't supported. We look foolish, and pushy. Pushiness is bothersome.

Goliath had foolhardy boldness in the face of David's ultimate power given by God. Goliath had become cocky, in fact, David's appearance made him over-confident. And that's what boldness is when it's unsupported, over confident, and underestimated: Goliath underestimated David, which is demonstrated here by Goliath:

1 Samuel 17:42-44

> *And when the Philistine looked about, and saw David, he disdained him: for he was but a youth, and ruddy, and of a fair*

CHAPTER 8: THE EIGHTH SON - THE OVER-CONFIDENT ONE

> *countenance. And the Philistine said unto David, Am I a dog, that thou comest to me with staves? And the Philistine cursed David by his gods. And the Philistine said to David, Come to me, and I will give thy flesh unto the fowls of the air, and to the beasts of the field.*

So Goliath made the first bold gesture. And he got a stone square in the forehead as a receipt.

Another example of rewarded boldness is the story of the woman whose boldness in following the Lord is touching example from Matthew 15:21-28:

Matthew 15:21-28

> *Then Jesus went thence, and departed into the coasts of Tyre and Sidon. And, behold, a woman of Canaan came out of the same coasts, and cried unto him, saying, Have mercy on me, O Lord, thou Son of David; my daughter is grievously vexed with a devil. But he answered her not a word. And his disciples came and besought him, saying, Send her away; for she crieth after us. But he answered and said, I am not sent but unto the lost sheep of the house of Israel. Then came she and worshipped him, saying, Lord, help me. But he answered and said, It is not meet to take the children's bread, and to cast it to dogs. And she said, Truth, Lord: yet the dogs eat of the crumbs which fall from their masters' table. Then Jesus answered and said unto her, O woman, great is thy faith: be it unto thee even as thou wilt. And her*

> *daughter was made whole from that very hour.*

Jesus rewarded the Canaanite woman's boldness because it was framed with her great faith in Him. There is also the story of the woman who touched the Lord's hem, who was instantly healed. It was bold of her to do that, and her desperation and faith made her bold.

Luke 8:22-47 contains the story where Jesus rewards this kind of boldness of the faithful:

Luke 8:22-48

> *Now it came to pass on a certain day, that he went into a ship with his disciples: and he said unto them, Let us go over unto the other side of the lake. And they launched forth. But as they sailed he fell asleep: and there came down a storm of wind on the lake; and they were filled with water, and were in jeopardy. And they came to him, and awoke him, saying, Master, master, we perish. Then he arose, and rebuked the wind and the raging of the water: and they ceased, and there was a calm. And he said unto them, Where is your faith? And they being afraid wondered, saying one to another, What manner of man is this! for he commandeth even the winds and water, and they obey him. And they arrived at the country of the Gadarenes, which is over against Galilee. And when he went forth to land, there met him out of the city a certain man, which had devils long time, and ware no clothes, neither abode in*

CHAPTER 8: THE EIGHTH SON - THE OVER-CONFIDENT ONE

any house, but in the tombs. When he saw Jesus, he cried out, and fell down before him, and with a loud voice said, What have I to do with thee, Jesus, thou Son of God most high? I beseech thee, torment me not. (For he had commanded the unclean spirit to come out of the man. For oftentimes it had caught him: and he was kept bound with chains and in fetters; and he brake the bands, and was driven of the devil into the wilderness.) And Jesus asked him, saying, What is thy name? And he said, Legion: because many devils were entered into him. And they besought him that he would not command them to go out into the deep. And there was there an herd of many swine feeding on the mountain: and they besought him that he would suffer them to enter into them. And he suffered them. Then went the devils out of the man, and entered into the swine: and the herd ran violently down a steep place into the lake, and were choked. When they that fed them saw what was done, they fled, and went and told it in the city and in the country. Then they went out to see what was done; and came to Jesus, and found the man, out of whom the devils were departed, sitting at the feet of Jesus, clothed, and in his right mind: and they were afraid. They also which saw it told them by what means he that was possessed of the devils was healed. Then the whole multitude of the country of the Gadarenes round about besought him to depart from them; for they were taken with great fear: and he went up into the ship, and returned back again. Now the man out of whom the devils were departed besought him that he might be with him: but Jesus sent him away, saying, Return to thine own house, and shew how great things God hath done unto thee. And he went his way, and published throughout the whole city how great things Jesus had done unto him. And it came to pass, that, when Jesus was returned, the people gladly received him: for they were all waiting for him. And, behold, there came a man named Jairus, and he was a ruler of the synagogue: and he fell down at Jesus' feet, and besought him that he would come into his house: For he had one only daughter, about twelve years of age, and she lay a dying. But as he went the people thronged him. And a woman having an issue of blood twelve years, which had spent all her living upon physicians, neither could be healed of any, Came behind him, and touched the border of his garment: and immediately her issue of blood stanched. And Jesus said, Who touched me? When all denied, Peter and they that were with him said, Master, the multitude throng thee and press thee, and sayest thou, Who touched me? And Jesus said, Somebody hath touched me: for I perceive that virtue is gone out of me. And when the woman saw that she was not hid, she came trembling, and falling down before him, she declared unto him before all the people for what cause she had touched him, and how she was healed immediately. And he said unto her, **Daughter, be of good comfort:**

CHAPTER 8: THE EIGHTH SON - THE OVER-CONFIDENT ONE

> ***thy faith hath made thee whole; go in peace.***

Isaiah 14:12-16

> *How art thou fallen from heaven, O Lucifer, son of the morning! how art thou cut down to the ground, which didst weaken the nations! For thou hast said in thine heart, I will ascend into heaven, I will exalt my throne above the stars of God: I will sit also upon the mount of the congregation, in the sides of the north: I will ascend above the heights of the clouds; I will be like the most High. Yet thou shalt be brought down to hell, to the sides of the pit. They that see thee shall narrowly look upon thee, and consider thee, saying, Is this the man that made the earth to tremble, that did shake kingdoms;*

What overconfidence! The arrogance and overconfidence of Satan is why he would even consider waging war against his very own Creator. He even thought he could tempt Jesus.

Man is even more overconfident if he thinks he can be immune to Satan, as the Evil One has been dealing with man for thousands of years and knows exactly how to manipulate and pull the wool over people's eyes: for the scripture says that Satan has fooled the whole world.

Revelation 12:9

> *And the great dragon was cast out, that old serpent, called the Devil, and Satan, which deceiveth the whole world: he was cast out*

into the earth, and his angels were cast out with him.

CHAPTER 9

The Ninth Son - The Arrogant One

Aridai means "dignified self" or "I am superior." It's the name of the ninth son of Haman to be killed, and then hanged. I try to remind myself that these things are such an abomination that Queen Esther wanted them killed and then hung for all to see.

Now there's a case to be made for the dignified self being something necessary and positive for ourselves and society. But when we overdignify ourselves, we become arrogant. And arrogance is just about at the very top of God's hate list.

Some people try to paint God as 'nothing but love.' Although everything God does is ultimately loving, that doesn't negate the fact that God has emotions and we are made in HIS image. So, does God hate? Yes. He does, and he hates arrogance (and pride, see Chapter 10) and here's proof:

Proverbs 8:13

> *The fear of the LORD is to hate evil: pride, and arrogancy, and the evil way, and the froward mouth, do I hate.*

By the way if you don't know, "froward" actually isn't forward, it means "perverse speech" although in our modern dictionaries it means "difficult to deal with, contrary" and I think also "divisive," as we see in the next passage the phrase "soweth discord among the brethren":

Proverbs 6:16-19

> *These six things doth the LORD hate: yea, seven are an abomination unto him: A proud look, a lying tongue, and hands that shed innocent blood, An heart that deviseth wicked imaginations, feet that be swift in running to mischief, A false witness that speaketh lies, and he that soweth discord among brethren.*

"A proud look." So what else does God hate besides arrogance? Pride. Self-righteousness (see Chapter 10).

This is one more thing to purge from the Christian personality that will please God. It's no wonder the ninth son of Haman bears this name.

We are to never be arrogant towards anyone, not just our Lord:

Philippians 2:3

> *Let nothing be done through strife or vainglory; but in lowliness of mind let each esteem other better than themselves.*

It's hard to be arrogant if we each "esteem other" (regard each other) better than ourselves!

CHAPTER 9: THE NINTH SON - THE ARROGANT ONE

Here are more statements about arrogance from the Word of God:

I Samuel 2:3

Talk no more so exceeding proudly; let not arrogancy come out of your mouth: for the LORD is a God of knowledge, and by him actions are weighed.

Isaiah 13:11

And I will punish the world for their evil, and the wicked for their iniquity; and I will cause the arrogancy of the proud to cease, and will lay low the haughtiness of the terrible.

Following is a wonderful story from the Bible about arrogance:

Luke 18:9-14

And he spake this parable unto certain which trusted in themselves that they were righteous, and despised others: Two men went up into the temple to pray; the one a Pharisee, and the other a publican. The Pharisee stood and prayed thus with himself, God, I thank thee, that I am not as other men are, extortioners, unjust, adulterers, or even as this publican. I fast twice in the week, I give tithes of all that I possess. And the publican, standing afar off, would not lift up so much as his eyes unto heaven, but smote upon his breast, saying, God be merciful to me a sinner. I tell you, this man went down to his house justified rather than the other:

> *for every one that exalteth himself shall be abased; and he that humbleth himself shall be exalted.*

From the popular website "Got Questions?" we read: "The Bible tells us those who are arrogant and have a haughty heart are an abomination to Him."

Proverbs 16:5.

> *Every one that is proud in heart is an abomination to the LORD: though hand join in hand, he shall not be unpunished.*

Of the seven things the Bible tells us that God hates, "haughty eyes" ["a proud look,"] is the first one listed (Proverbs 6:16-19).

Isaiah 2:17-18

> *And the loftiness of man shall be bowed down, and the haughtiness of men shall be made low: and the LORD alone shall be exalted in that day. And the idols he shall utterly abolish.*

Jeremiah 48:29-30

> *We have heard the pride of Moab, (he is exceeding proud) his loftiness, and his arrogancy, and his pride, and the haughtiness of his heart. I know his wrath, saith the LORD; but it shall not be so; his lies shall not so effect it.*

God keeps man humble in various ways:

CHAPTER 9: THE NINTH SON - THE ARROGANT ONE

1 Corinthians 1:27

> *But God hath chosen the foolish things of the world to confound the wise; and God hath chosen the weak things of the world to confound the things which are mighty;*

Isaiah 2:11 also tells us the outcome for the arrogant:

Isaiah 2:11

> *The lofty looks of man shall be humbled, and the haughtiness of men shall be bowed down, and the LORD alone shall be exalted in that day.*

God is humble, which is why Jesus is humble, because He is God's Son, the perfect image of the invisible God (Colossians 1:15). And He will put an end to all the arrogant:

Isaiah 13:11

> *And I will punish the world for their evil, and the wicked for their iniquity; and I will cause the arrogancy of the proud to cease, and will lay low the haughtiness of the terrible.*

Here's another great story about the fate of an arrogant king:

Daniel 5:18-23

> *O thou king, the most high God gave Nebuchadnezzar thy father a kingdom, and majesty, and glory, and honour: And for the majesty that he gave him, all people,*

nations, and languages, trembled and feared before him: whom he would he slew; and whom he would he kept alive; and whom he would he set up; and whom he would he put down. But when his heart was lifted up, and his mind hardened in pride, he was deposed from his kingly throne, and they took his glory from him: And he was driven from the sons of men; and his heart was made like the beasts, and his dwelling was with the wild asses: they fed him with grass like oxen, and his body was wet with the dew of heaven; till he knew that the most high God ruled in the kingdom of men, and that he appointeth over it whomsoever he will. And thou his son, O Belshazzar, hast not humbled thine heart, though thou knewest all this; But hast lifted up thyself against the Lord of heaven; and they have brought the vessels of his house before thee, and thou, and thy lords, thy wives, and thy concubines, have drunk wine in them; and thou hast praised the gods of silver, and gold, of brass, iron, wood, and stone, which see not, nor hear, nor know: and the God in whose hand thy breath is, and whose are all thy ways, hast thou not glorified:

Nimrod had all the earthly gifts that God could bestow and yet didn't praise the real and living God for all that was given to him. And for his arrogance, God struck down the Tower of Babel.

CHAPTER 10

The Tenth Son - The Pharisee

Luke 18:9-14

> *And he spake this parable unto certain which trusted in themselves that they were righteous, and despised others: Two men went up into the temple to pray; the one a Pharisee, and the other a publican. The Pharisee stood and prayed thus with himself, God, I thank thee, that I am not as other men are, extortioners, unjust, adulterers, or even as this publican. I fast twice in the week, I give tithes of all that I possess. And the publican, standing afar off, would not lift up so much as his eyes unto heaven, but smote upon his breast, saying, God be merciful to me a sinner. I tell you, this man went down to his house justified rather than the other: for every one that exalteth himself shall be abased; and he that humbleth himself shall be exalted.*

The most angry Jesus became with anyone was with the Pharisees. And the Pharisees promoted the torture and death of the very Messiah they had been waiting for. They didn't recognize Him even when He told them to their face, I am HE.

The Pharisees and the Sadducees were allegedly the most religious people, and widely regarded as the most biblically knowledgeable people of the time. Yet they hated Jesus, the perfect image of the Creator who was fulfilling their very own scriptures. And Jesus hated them from what we see that He called them: vipers, sons of the devil, and He told them unless they would believe that Jesus was He, who He said He was, who He claimed to be, the great I Am, that they would die in their sins. He said, *"If ye were Abraham's children, ye would do the works of Abraham."*

The last name of the sons of Haman is "Vajezatha," which means "pure self" or "self-righteous," and it's as though Our Father saved the best for last. One can see two different aspects from these two meanings from the outset.

First is that pure self would be simple selfishness, and the second would be the self-righteous aspect which we know that the Pharisees and Sadducees greatly were.

Jesus also taught against self-righteous praying, fasting, charity, and other practices. For instance, being loud when praying so others can hear you, announcing your donations to the poor, making hungry grimace while fasting so that others can see what you're doing is painful, this is making earthly reward for yourself, and that is all - instead of the rewards you can expect in Heaven. Your rewards on earth are all you would get.

CHAPTER 10: THE TENTH SON - THE ARROGANT PHARISEE

Rather, these practices are to be done in a holy fashion. The Lord tells us to go to a private place and pray in secret.

Matthew 6:3

> *But when thou doest alms, let not thy left hand know what thy right hand doeth:*

Matthew 6:6

> *But thou, when thou prayest, enter into thy closet, and when thou hast shut thy door, pray to thy Father which is in secret; and thy Father which seeth in secret shall reward thee openly.*

The Lord wants no one to give under compulsion; He wants a "cheerful giver."

The Pharisees were law keepers, and wanted everyone under the yoke of the Law, *and their interpretation of it*. They thought better of themselves than others. They were pretentious and sanctimonious. That's what Jesus said He didn't want, *"Lest any man should boast."*

The Pharisees self-righteously looked down upon people and hated Jesus for setting them free from their rules and hence, their control. So at their pleading they were ultimately responsible for Jesus' death upon the cross at the hands of the Romans. They spent a lot of time following Jesus around accusing Him of anything they could, such as breaking Sabbath or being a wine-bibber.

They paid Judas in silver, His own follower, to arrange for Jesus' arrest. The charge was blasphemy; that *"He maketh Himself God"* (proof that Jesus made it clear that He is God in the Flesh). Of course, we all know Judas regretted his action after Jesus' crucifixion. He threw the silver back at the Pharisees and committed suicide. The Pharisees used the money to buy his burial plot. Some say Judas was repentant; others say he was never saved. Where self-righteousness leads is very dismal.

Self-righteousness is distasteful because it shows the person who acts this way has denied those who should get the credit:

John 15:5

> *I am the vine, ye are the branches: He that abideth in me, and I in him, the same bringeth forth much fruit: for without me ye can do nothing.*

When we're self-righteous, we believe we're better than others, and can cast the first stone as if we have no sin. We all have sin:

Romans 3:22-28

> *Even the righteousness of God which is by faith of Jesus Christ unto all and upon all them that believe: for there is no difference: For all have sinned, and come short of the glory of God; Being justified freely by his grace through the redemption that is in Christ Jesus: Whom God hath set forth to be*

CHAPTER 10: THE TENTH SON - THE ARROGANT PHARISEE

> *a propitiation through faith in his blood, to declare his righteousness for the remission of sins that are past, through the forbearance of God; To declare, I say, at this time his righteousness: that he might be just, and the justifier of him which believeth in Jesus. Where is boasting then? It is excluded. By what law? of works? Nay: but by the law of faith. Therefore we conclude that a man is justified by faith without the deeds of the law.*

This was terrible news to the law keepers, the Pharisees! No wonder they hated Jesus so.

Self-righteousness also implies that we can judge others. If we all sin, how can we do that? The Bible warns us to be very careful when judging someone else and teaches us to *"judge righteously."*

Matthew 7:1-5

> *Judge not, that ye be not judged. For with what judgment ye judge, ye shall be judged: and with what measure ye mete, it shall be measured to you again. And why beholdest thou the mote that is in thy brother's eye, but considerest not the beam that is in thine own eye? Or how wilt thou say to thy brother, Let me pull out the mote out of thine eye; and, behold, a beam is in thine own eye? Thou hypocrite, first cast out the beam out of thine own eye; and then shalt thou see clearly to cast out the mote out of thy brother's eye.*

Count your own sins before you count anyone else's. It helps to keep you humble, and from falling into the trap of being self-righteous before God, and becoming a "Vajezatha," the very last name of the ten sons of Haman, who was killed and then hung twice in history.

EPILOGUE

The ten sons of Haman manifest the sinful natures of the enemies of God, hidden inside each of their individual Hebrew names. But these traits also occur in all human beings to some degree. It's a substantial list of things to work on, for anyone who loves the Lord, and is maturing in their own godly nature. God encloses some wonderful secrets inside His Word to help anyone, and for those who want to counsel others regarding their emotional life, this list is a nice set of tools.

But this is just the beginning of what God can show us in His Word about how to counsel well. Jesus is "Wonderful, Counselor" as His first description when reading Isaiah 9.

Isaiah 9:6

> *For unto us a child is born, unto us a son is given: and the government shall be upon his shoulder: and his name shall be called Wonderful, Counseller, The mighty God, The everlasting Father, The Prince of Peace.*

Whether you are a professional or a layman, God has blessed us abundantly with His gift of truth, through scripture, that shapes our spirit natures, as human beings. He shows us the things that need to change within all human nature because all of us are guilty of these ten sinful natures, at some point. This includes ourselves, as counselors.

THE PSYCHOLOGY OF GOD: TEN SONS OF HAMAN

We must keep looking at the Bible, and digging. Passages hide within the scriptures that are 'keys' for change within ourselves that will bring us closer to what God wants for us as His children. Jesus is the ultimate physician and healer and He has given us this Word as a blessing, as children of God, especially those who are in the business of helping people with their "psychological state."

There are many more Bible stories throughout scripture that have deeper meaning; that demonstrate psychological issues, problems and solutions, as God holds up the mirror to man. For instance, why did Adam blame Eve, instead of taking responsibility for his own actions? Why did Samson allow such a sinful woman into his life? Why did Cain kill his brother? Examples run through the entire Bible. There's a lot more to teach us under the surface story; the deeper human experience hidden underneath.

This is precisely what we are trying to accomplish within the series The Psychology of God. Allowing God to direct us in how to heal what ails the human mind and spirit by digging into the scripture to find the meaning it contains. Gifts of wisdom, hidden like Easter eggs, as we seek God's face.

We are told to love God with all our mind, heart, and strength. The Lord wants not only our bodies to be free from sin and unblemished, but especially our hearts and minds.

EPILOGUE

How can we not marvel at the eternal, consistent nature of what we learn from the Word of God, which never changes? As we look at these "keys" to human nature, inside the Bible, what I see is eternal truth; we cannot compare "man's knowledge" to God's; it becomes pale. Today, Sigmund Freud and others are mocked; while all over the Bible, everlasting wisdom and clues to our eternal joy, and even solutions to life's problems today are given away, free. It isn't an 'antiquated' book as some think. *The attributes found in the ten sons of Haman are the same sinful ways in 4000 BC, as they are in 2018. And the cure is still the same.*

Where we go from here, with all the wonderful possibilities and opportunities given inside the scriptures, will be up to those practitioners and researchers who respect the Word of God enough to continue this journey, to find what God wants for His people.

Thank you for reading my book.

LM McCormick

INDEX OF WORDS AND PHRASES

Abel, 82
Abigail, 57, 58
Adalia, 17, 65
adversity, 41
Amalek, 14
Amalekites, 14
ambitious, 17, 85
Ananias, 57, 86, 87
anger, 7, 39, 40, 61, 67, 88
antithesis, 6
Aridai, 17, 103
Aridatha, 17, 73
Arisai, 17, 93
arrogance, 101, 103-105, 108
artifacts, 27
Aspatha, 17, 47, 49
assertiveness, 17, 79
attributes, 15, 53, 94, 117
autonomous, 48
Babylon, 63
bitterness, 40, 61
black arts, 21
blasphemy, 25, 112
bold, 5, 69, 73, 82, 93, 94, 97, 98
boldness, 93-98
bully, 5, 74
busybody, 17, 19, 20

Cain, 82, 85, 116
complaining, 39, 40
confused, 7, 67
Creator, 7, 32, 57, 101, 110
Curious, 17, 19, 21
cyanide, 15
D.H. Lawrence, 42
dabbling, 21
Dalphon, 17, 37
David, 31, 32, 41, 58, 69, 95-97
demons, 26, 27
depressed, 7, 37, 41, 49
depression, 7, 42, 44
description, 6, 60, 63, 115
drugs, 22
drunkenness, 22
education, 8
enemies, 5, 15, 16, 19, 57, 75, 115
Esau, 14, 88
Esther, 5, 13-16, 103
evil, 6, 8, 13, 15, 27, 39, 53, 56, 61, 70, 79, 81, 86, 88, 90, 91, 103, 105, 107
failure, 8, 16
Generous, 17

Goliath, 69, 95-97
gossiping, 5, 18
guilt, 7, 40
Haman, 1, 5-8, 13-15, 17-19, 37, 42, 47, 53, 65, 73, 74, 82, 85, 94, 103, 104, 110, 114, 115, 117
haughty, 17, 106
headstrong, 5
healing, 5, 7
Henrietta Newton Martin, 45
Hinduism, 26
Hollywood, 21
Horus, 24
human nature, 6, 7, 115, 117
humility, 5, 51, 63, 66-68
independence, 48, 53
inferiority, 17
insight, 7
Jabez, 89
Jezebel, 26, 59, 87, 88
Job, 39
Jonah, 74-78
Judas, 53, 57, 89, 112
judge, 19, 113
Karma, 51
knowledge, 5, 8, 19, 93, 105, 117
Lazarus, 33, 55

Le Vey, 21
lost, 7, 97
Lot, 62, 74, 79, 80-82
love, 3, 6, 8, 38, 43, 59, 65, 70, 82, 90, 91, 103, 116
mankind, 6, 21, 82
marriage, 23
Mordecai, 13, 16
Moses, 56, 57, 66, 67
Nabal, 57, 58
names, 5, 6, 15-19, 53, 73, 115
narcissism, 85
Nazi, 15
Nebuchadnezzar, 107
negativity, 18
Nuremberg, 14, 15
occult, 21, 24
paganism, 23
Parmashta, 17, 85
Parshandatha, 17
Peace symbol, 22
personality, 5, 15, 18, 19, 37, 53, 55, 65, 85, 87, 104
Pharisees, 25, 33, 57, 60, 89, 109, 110-113
Poratha, 17, 53
prayer, 6, 39, 89
Preeminent, 17
prescription, 8, 40
prideful, 17, 62
prodigal, 59

INDEX OF WORDS AND PHRASES

prophecies, 7, 32, 43
psychological, 18, 53, 74, 116
Psychology Today, 48
Rabbi, 14
rebellious, 22
sad sack, 37
salt, 62, 81
salvation, 7, 30, 41, 70, 78, 83
Sapphira, 57, 86, 87
secrets, 7, 9, 115
secularism, 23
self-consciousness, 17
self-indulgence, 17, 53-55, 59, 60, 62, 63
self-righteousness, 17, 18, 112
self-sufficiency, 17, 47, 48
signs, 29, 32, 34
snakes, 26
Sodom, 62, 63, 79-82
soothsayers, 28, 29
sorrow, 8, 42
spend-thriftiness, 17
Stephen Fry, 44
superiority, 17

temptations, 6, 22
Tom Robbins, 44
traits, 5, 6, 18, 65, 115
trust, 7, 50, 54, 69, 70
truth, 8, 22-25, 47, 61, 67, 81, 115, 117
UFO, 27
unconditionally, 7
Vajezatha, 17, 110, 114
Weak, 17
Weeping, 17, 37
Word, 6-8, 19, 22, 23, 32, 38, 39, 47, 50, 54, 65, 69, 74, 81, 83, 86, 94, 105, 115-117

ABOUT THE AUTHOR

LM McCormick has been an American advertising copywriter for the last 35 years, and recently turned her attention to writing for God. She loves cooking, her two golden retrievers, her family, and most of all, our Lord Jesus Christ. LM has an affection for apologetics; scientific, historical, and political study; facts that prove God's existence, and help us understand the physical world He designed for us. She regularly engages in debates centering on the fables of evolution, false religions, and the mental illness of atheism. The author holds an undergraduate degree in psychology from the University of Washington, and a master's degree in organizational communication from Purdue University, with a focus on semiotics.

www.ingramcontent.com/pod-product-compliance
Lightning Source LLC
LaVergne TN
LVHW051601080426
835510LV00020B/3078